NATURE STORIES

DEPICTIONS OF THE ENVIRONMENT AND THEIR EFFECTS

THE HAMPTON PRESS COMMUNICATION SERIES
Communication Alternatives
Brenda Dervin, supervisory editor

The Reach of Dialogue: Confirmation, Voice and Community
  Rob Anderson, Kenneth N. Cissna, and Ronald C. Arnett (eds.)

Desert Storm and the Mass Media
  Bradley S. Greenberg and Walter Gantz (eds.)

Responsible Communication: Ethical Issues in Business, Industry,
  and the Professions
  James A. Jaksa and Michael S. Pritchard (eds.)

Communication and Trade: Essays in Honor of
  Meheroo Jussawalla
  Donald Lamberton (ed.)

Public Intimacies: Talk Show Participants and Tell-All TV
  Patricia Joyner Priest

Nature Stories: Depictions of the Environment and Their Effects
  James Shanahan and Katherine McComas

forthcoming

Liberating Alternatives: The Founding Convention of the Cultural
  Environment Movement
  Kate Duncan (ed.)

Theorizing Fandom: Fans, Subcultures, and Identity
  Cheryl Harris and Alison Alexander (eds.)

U.S. Glasnost: Missing Political Themes in U.S. Media Discourse
  Johan Galtung and Richard Vincent

Communication and Development: The Freirean Connection
  Michael Richards, Pradip N. Thomas and Zaharom Nain (eds.)

Hearing Muted Voices
  Anita Taylor and M.J. Hardman (eds.)

NATURE STORIES

DEPICTIONS OF THE ENVIRONMENT AND THEIR EFFECTS

James Shanahan
Katherine McComas

Cornell University

HAMPTON PRESS, INC.
CRESSKILL, NEW JERSEY

Printed in the United State of America

Library of Congress Cataloging-in-Publication Data

Shanahan, James
   Nature stories : depictions of the environment and their effects / James Shanahan, Katherine McComas.
      p. cm. -- (The Hampton Press communication series)
   Includes bibliographical references and index.
   ISBN 1-57273-200-8 (cl.). -- ISBN 1-57273-201-6 (pbk.)
   1. Environmentalism. 2. Nature--Effect of human beings on.
3. Philosophy of nature.   I. McComas, Katherine. II. Title.
III. Series.
GE195.S46   1998
363.7--dc21   98-30187
                                                                  CIP

Hampton Press, Inc.
23 Broadway
Cresskill, NJ 07626

to Sheldon Wappler and Bess Shale

CONTENTS

ACKNOWLEDGMENTS

There are many individuals who have contributed to this book, although of course we retain responsibility for its conclusions. I began work on it while teaching at Boston University. The helpful advice and friendship of colleagues such as Julie Dobrow, Tobe Berkovitz, Alan Holliday, Walter Lubars, and Larry Martin were much appreciated. The contributions of graduate students such as Anniken Naess were also very important. It is also at Boston University where I first met Katherine McComas, who as co-author has provided the much needed energy and perspective to finish the book.

On moving to Cornell, we have encountered many other fine colleagues who have helped us refine our thinking about these issues. Bruce Lewenstein, Cliff Scherer, Dan McDonald, and Carroll Glynn deserve credit for their collegiality and insight. Colleagues in the natural resources department such as Dan Decker have also been very helpful. Lisa Pelstring, a Cornell graduate student, has contributed enormously, especially to the content analysis work.

Also, I thank Michael Morgan at the University of Massachusetts for his continued collaboration and inspiration. George Gerbner, Nancy Signorielli, L. J. Shrum, and other colleagues in the cultural indicators research community also provided a great deal of inspiration.

I thank Brenda Dervin, who provided much needed editorial perspective. Thanks to two anonymous reviewers who improved the manuscript immensely. Also, many thanks to Barbara Bernstein of Hampton Press for providing a hospitable and rewarding publishing environment.

Finally, to Lisa and Isabel, I continue to say thanks in every way I can think of.

James Shanahan

* * * * *

Foremost, to Jim Shanahan, who as a mentor and a friend has offered years of support and wisdom, I am grateful you had the confidence in me to bring me on board this worthwhile project.

I thank the countless faculty and friends at Boston University and Cornell University who have stimulated my mind and helped me grow as a scholar and a person.

I send our sincere gratitude for thoughtful, useful comments to the reviewers of earlier drafts of this manuscript.

Finally, to my family and loved ones, you are my strength and my reward.

Katherine McComas

one

INTRODUCTION

This book is about relationships between stories, people, and their environments. In particular, we focus on the role played by the mass media, especially television. Although there have been a few studies of the role of television in environmental narratives (see chapter 2 for a comprehensive review), few have taken an explicitly narrative perspective; rather, research tends to favor an approach that sees mass media as distributing "information." Working from a critical and empirical position, we examine how mass media institutions have constructed the environmental issue through narrative. We also examine how publics have responded to these narratives. Without discounting the important role that the dissemination of information plays in environmental communication, our approach places a great deal of weight on the "fictional" environment created by the modern mass media.

This is a rather broad topic, so it is important to be clear about the real focus: We are interested in the function of narratives in our understanding of nature, and the kinds of impacts these narratives can have on the environment. Beyond that, we establish what role and functions these narratives play for us and for our social system. In essence, we establish the boundaries for a theory of mass media's contribution to environmental understanding. Building on extensive previous research from communication scholars on the communication of environmental information, we apply concepts from the literature on narrative and subsume these within an overarching theory of mass communication: the theory of "cultivation." This multifaceted project must, perforce, be exploratory, but it has its own merits. Such a project allows for linkages to be developed in ways that have never been tried, particularly in tying theory of narrative to an empirically based critical theory of mass communication.

THE RELATIONSHIP BETWEEN THE HUMAN AND THE NATURAL ENVIRONMENT

Certainly our stories are important to how we "interpret" nature. But *nature* is itself a social construct. Nature is part of a social reality and can "speak" back to us from its position as a social entity. The things we say about the environment, the stories we tell about it, and the culture we erect within it have a significant impact on the reactions we experience from nature. Backes (1995) noted that environmental and human social "systems are linked, not by geography or by mechanical or biological laws, but by human perceptions of and behavior toward the ecosystem" (p. 150).

We assume that the environment can be understood not only as a physical fact but as a social construct. That, of course, is not a new idea.[1] Almost all fields of human endeavor, including music, poetry, literature, drama, art, and social criticism have dealt in important ways with the relationship between people and nature. Sometimes we demonize nature, as in the "dread" wilderness of the American pioneers. Other times we idealize it, as in the Romantic poets or the "Appalachian Spring" of Aaron Copland. Sometimes, nature can be a powerful character in a drama, as in Moby Dick, whereas other approaches have tended to make nature recede into the background, as in the drawing room comedy or today's television sitcom. Nature can be molded to fit our narrative purposes.

Beyond this, there is an appearance of "consciousness" to the environment, both in the way we think about it and in the way

---

[1]For instance, White (1967), in a much cited essay, discussed early notions of nature as a resource, seeing these notions as emerging from Biblical sources. Others (e.g., Nash, 1982) have noted the fact that early American approaches to wilderness were imbued with a strong element of fear and contempt.

we attribute consciousness to it (as, for instance, in the Gaia hypothesis of Lovelock, 1995). If there is an aspect of consciousness to the environment, then the project of this book seems natural: a discussion of how the stories we tell about the environment interweave with the environment itself, and what we get out of the relationship. This discussion can lead to an answer to the overall question of how these stories help us to create a climate to protect or to encourage us to harm nature.

ENVIRONMENTAL AND NARRATIVE SYSTEMS

Today, the environment seems to demand our attention more than ever before. Perhaps this is a natural development, given the fact that human growth at some point must push against the limits of its context. It may simply be that we do not notice our walls until we are literally crammed against them by the outward push of progress. Or, one may argue that human population is a long way from its upper limit (Simon, 1995), and so our fascination with the environment must be motivated by some other force. It could be that significant leisure time has produced opportunity for cultivating a finer pursuit such as environmentalism. Another argument is that the effects of our story-telling activities have revealed an environmental "deficiency," that we must attempt to repair through narrative work.

In order to explain interactions between our story-telling activities and the environment, we appropriate a systems analogy. The environment itself is, obviously, a kind of system. Human society is another kind of system. Human interactions obviously take place within the context of the environment. A logical conclusion might therefore be that the environment is a higher order system than is human society, that human society is only one component of a much larger natural system with many more levels of complexity and interaction than are possible within the simpler human system.

On the physical level, it would seem to be difficult to deny such a conclusion. In material terms, we are contained and always, already contexted by our physical environment. But there is another level at which human systems have the ability to transcend their environment. The nature of social activity is such that we have the capacity, indeed the drive, to "build" our own environments. Through language, communication, narrative, and so forth, we become literally *homo faber*, the species that makes.

Thus, there is something of a systemic paradox. The paradox can be reduced to two partially contradictory propositions:

Proposition 1: Human society is always materially contexted by its physical environment.
Proposition 2: Human society is not always socially contexted by its physical environment.

In Proposition 2, we are tempted to argue that human society is "never" socially contexted by its environment, although it is
hard to ignore the obvious impacts of climate, geography, available
resources, and so forth, on the development of cultures. Still, the
conclusion that social activity allows us the opportunity to "escape"
our material conditions is quite defensible. Assuming that social
reality is almost as "durable" as physical reality, the emerging paradox can only be solved by assuming that human society exists in at
least two spheres, the natural and the social. How these realities
are made to interact with each other is then a key question.

One way of dealing with the paradox is that seen in recent
developments in social theory, favoring "relativist" positions on the
nature of reality, which make it difficult to even conceive of an
objectively existing environment. On this view, everything is a
"text," and all texts permit multiple readings. We see this, however,
as a radical formulation. Although the communicational activities
of humans have increasingly and properly been seen to be enormously powerful, whether we can, through communication, escape
our environmental context "permanently" is a question that begs an
answer. At some point, the physical reality of the environment
places demands that must be satisfied on human-constructed symbolic environments. Still, at any given point in time, it may "appear"
that the human-constructed environments are more powerfully real
than objective physical realities. In order to achieve this feat,
human conceptions and constructions of environment must deal
with systemic complexity in a variety of ways.

We assume that, from a systemic perspective, "nature" is a
higher order system than "humans," because nature contains
humans as a systemic component. Whatever we do as humans may
well be unpredictable and complex, but that is only one factor in
the greater complexity of nature. Thus, to predict and explain the
environment is to explain something more complex than ourselves.
Increasing systemic complexity forces us to rely on "constructs"
that can simplify matters, bringing them within human control.
Many of these constructs turn out to be narrative, a type of system
over which we as humans can exert control because narrative systems are of a lesser order than the humans who create them.

Of course, we have not always realized this fact. Many cultures and ideologies have proposed that Nature really is sub-
servient to Man, and therefore its greater complexity and "higher"

natural status has been ignored. But the axiom of the unpredictability of a natural system ("you can never do just one thing") is beginning to settle into the broad Western consciousness, revealing the poverty of a human narrative perspective that excludes nature. Now, at least, some of us are understanding not that Nature has limits (which is also true) but that we as humans have these limits. Although human society, as lower level subsystem, can obviously produce feedbacks into the suprasystem of the environment, it can never become the context for the environment itself.

At least one face of the environment must be its objectivity. Inescapably, whatever we think about the environment cannot conceivably bc sophisticated enough to understand all of it; there will always be factors we fail to take into account, and our plans will always be imperfect. That does not mean that we will not find ways to "manage" within this environment; evolution gears us to a certain extent for this task. But as environmental planners, we tend to fail. Perhaps somewhat ironically, this amplifies the importance of social conceptions. Precisely because we cannot completely nor scientifically understand all of the environment as a system, we tend to rely increasingly on social and cultural conceptions. That is because we can comprehensively understand and control, and live within, narrative understandings.

To use another metaphor, one may conceive of the human conception of the environment as a rocket that cannot escape the gravitational pull of the objective reality of the natural environment. Although we can power ourselves on fanciful flights, reconceptualizing nature as we go, the reality of the physical environment will inevitably tend to pull us back. Any narrative will have to deal with this gravitational pull. In the long term, this narrative gravity exerts a stronger force than our social energies. Still, the orbits can be long-lasting.

Global warming can be used as a case study. Some have recently claimed that greenhouse warming has the potential to be the next doomsday agent. *Time* wailed that

> according to computer projections, the accumulation of CO_2 could drive up the planet's average temperature 3° F to 9° F by the middle of the next century. That could cause the oceans to rise several feet, flooding coastal areas and ruining huge tracts of farmland through salinization. Changing weather patterns could make huge areas infertile or uninhabitable, touching off refugee movements unprecedented in history. ("Planet of the year," p. 28)

McKibben (1989), a recent popularizer of environmental problems, devoted all of his *The End of Nature* to the aesthetics and ethics of this problem. In a remarkable piece of writing, McKibben won undoubted new support for the fear of global warming. From this perspective, global warming has the potential to wipe out everything we now understand to be natural and dear to us. The oceans may rise, crops may die, entire peoples could disappear; everything would be different.

Or maybe we would adapt. Or maybe the globe will not warm. Who really knows? Actually, the most sophisticated scientist cannot claim with any final accuracy to know when and if the globe will warm, or what will really and truly cause such a rise, if it does come. Although recent reports by the Intergovernmental Panel on Climate Change claim human causality in the global warming arena, others disagree. For instance, S. Singer (1992), a climate scientist said:

> we cannot be sure whether the next century will bring a warming that is negligible or a warming that is significant . . . even if there is a global warming and associated climate changes, it is debatable whether the consequences will be good or bad; likely we would get some of each. (p. 394)

It may be that Singer is a charlatan, or that *Time* magazine is a propaganda rag, or that McKibben is a dupe. Whatever the "real" case, faced with such uncertainty, the "average person" has little ground for concrete action or belief. One can conclude that the purpose of such a narrative is to confuse, or to entertain, or to inform, but to base action on such communication is difficult. From a practical social perspective, the concept of global warming is a fiction, albeit a narratively strong invention. Recent hot summers give the story credence, but for most people it is still a "story."

In the end, most of us can only base our actions on a story. Of course, some fictions are useful, others harmful. The practices we indulge in certainly have a bearing on the issue, even if we cannot be certain what they are. If we continue to spew greenhouse gases, isn't that important? Undoubtedly it is. We're just not sure how important. If we stopped spewing greenhouse gases, would that save us in the long run? Maybe it would, but who would bet his or her lifestyle on it? The fact is, this pressing environmental problem is understood about as little as most of the large-scale environmental problems we face today. Ozone holes, population issues, chemical pollution, resource depletion, land conservation, wildlife preservation, and virtually any environmental issue are understood by mass audiences in relatively small ways, mostly through environmental narratives.

The environmental stories we choose to believe will generally be those of the most utility. Stories that radically threaten our identity will be eventually discarded, even if they temporarily serve purposes of diversion and entertainment. When we have little factual basis for our actions (which is much of the time), we tend to fall back on ideologies and belief systems. Furthermore, even when we do have a factual basis, it is strongly contexted by our "nonfactual" and narrative information. This means that what we "think" about the environment is in many ways much more important than what we "know" about it. Environmental popularizers, television programmers, and nature evangelists are probably much more important than many would think in determining our "knowledge" about the environment. That is another basis for this study, which examines underlying social bases for modern day environmentalism, with an emphasis on the cultural and narrative aspects.

Of course science is not without effect. The teachings of our accumulated environmental science do have an important higher level lesson. We have managed to gain a meta-understanding that human management generally generates consequences that will not be understood. We have learned from particular disasters that others may well result if we are too enthusiastic in our technological gymnastics. We can see the now common feeling that humans are not really part of nature as part of this understanding; we are instead coming to see ourselves as nature's principal enemy. But this message depends as much on our now common stories of Man as environmental despoiler as they do on scientific research demonstrating any facts relevant to the issue. What we do has consequences, and there always seems to be the possibility of ramifications beyond our understanding. Of course, technologies as varied as the wheel, fire, the water mill, penicillin, and many others have positively improved human life without harming the environment in a significant way. Clearly, few would argue that human agency should be abandoned as a way of preserving environmental or our own health. But many of the consequences we do not understand tend to have dire implications; ecology tells us that we can never do just one thing, and the rules under which the ecological and evolutionary game is played mean that poorly understood consequences are likely to have harmful rather than helpful impacts.

Thus, a primary environmental problem today is uncertainty. We cannot say for certain what will happen, although we sometimes think we have the technologies to permit such predictions to be made. The problem is one of magnitude. No matter how globally we examine the problem, there is always more to analyze, and even below the global level the problems quickly become chaotic. The environment, not religion, is rapidly becoming today's principal area of uncertainty and therefore a most important source for discussions about the meaning of life. It is not surprising, then, that mythologies of environmentalism are appearing to reduce this uncertainty. "Adherents" to environmentalism need not be scientists; they need simply to have narratively formed concepts about the right thing to do, that environmentalism is a healthier way of life than say, Fabian socialism or orthodox neoclassical liberalism. Environmental preachers such as Muir, Leopold, Carson, Cousteau, and McKibben bring a message of wholeness and meaning to a chaotic world of scientific uncertainty.

The physical environment, then, is a complex system evolving in ways we can rarely completely understand. Certainly, narrative constructions of the environment present a much easier challenge for human understanding. At some level, what we think and say about the environment really becomes almost more important than the environment itself, in the sense that what objectively happens in the world (which fuels we use, which gases get spewed, etc.) is a function of which ideology wins the battle. The human technology for disseminating ideology is narrative.

RECENT ENVIRONMENTAL DEBATES AND NARRATIVE DIMENSIONS OF ENVIRONMENTALISM

As with any good story, there are lots of different versions and different ways to tell it. As of 1998, many separate environmental stories have sprung into existence; it is no longer simply a question of whether one supports "growth" or "conservation." Clearly, a major dimension of environmentalism still involves the question of whether society should continue to grow rapidly, but this is a continuum, with some believing that growth can be "sustainable," whereas others assert that growth itself is perverse. And, of course, a significant majority still subscribe to the notion that growth itself is a desirable goal.

The growth aspect of environmentalism is connected to how anthropocentric one's conception is. Some environmentalists would argue that the environment should be "conserved" because that is what makes the most sense from a human perspective. We conserve "resources" so we can have them to use later. On the other hand, there are those who defend the environment simply because it is "worth" defending. This debate is as old as environmentalism itself, extending back to the debate between John Muir and Gifford Pinchot (Fox, 1985).

The anthropocentric dimension of environmentalism has been identified as a key issue by those writers who have proposed a "new environmental paradigm" (Dunlap & VanLiere, 1984). The old paradigm (we discuss this in more detail later) is simply the ideology that emphasizes human dominion over nature, including the Judeo-Christian directive to multiply and use nature and all God's creatures for Man's purposes. This ideology still, obviously, survives intact among a strong majority of Westerners. This human-centered view is strongly characteristic certainly of basic everyday Western social reality and characterizes the life practices of not a few environmentalists as well. Certainly, environmental "optimists" (a new strain represented by Easterbrook, 1995) partake liberally of old paradigm thinking, tinged by the belief that technology will produce environmental benefits to counteract the problems. Environmentalism itself has often been characterized as an anti-Christian pro-Communist crusade among adherents to this ideology.

Rejecting anthropocentrism seems a sufficient, if not a necessary condition, to qualifying as a "true environmentalist." Anyone who claims to put his or her own self-interest aside in favor of the rights or interests of other species or nature certainly would count as a kind of environmentalist. Indeed, most debates in recent work on environmental ethics center on this issue of human rights versus "other" rights. Rodman (1983), for instance, identifies two basic values inherent in this "other-directed" dimension of environmentalism. One is that

> one ought not to treat with disrespect or use as a mere means anything that has a telos or end of its own—anything that is autonomous in the basic sense of having a capacity for internal self-direction and self-regulation. (cited in VanDeVeer & Pierce, 1986, p. 166)

This may be a rather harsh criterion for what environmentalist behavior might hope to achieve. After all, the smallest flea or slimiest oyster seems to meet these criteria; even minute microbes might. Should all behavior by humans meet a test of respect for such things? Probably not, but this position, as a building member for the superstructure of environmentalism, seems essential in some form. The lesson of stories with this feature is that "rights" adhere to almost everything.

The second value, which we call the *systems value*, is the tendency to give worth to entities that have the characteristics of diversity, complexity, integrity, harmony, stability, scarcity, etc. While the telos principle serves primarily to provide a common basic reason for respectful treatment of natural entities and natural systems . . . , this cluster of value-giving qualities provides criteria for evaluating alternative courses of permissible action in terms of optimizing the production of good effects, the better action being the one that optimizes the qualities taken as an interdependent, mutually constraining cluster. (p.167)

As an example, a cow monoculture might be considered less environmentally worthy than a diverse stream ecosystem in the vicinity of a farm. Using this dimension, the environmentalist would argue to protect the stream from the cows and not vice versa, even though both systems can be argued to display a telos. Thus, entities with competing rights can be evaluated according to this criterion.

So contemporary environmentalism may be seen as the set of stories and beliefs encouraging conservation, nonanthropocentrism, and the systems value. But in order to properly understand environmentalism, we also need to correctly understand its practical aspects, both from the perspective of public opinion and from the ideological perspective. Environmentalism is not simply an ideology, it is also a practice. Most people "say" they are environmentalist (Gillroy & Shapiro, 1986), at least if one asks them in a public opinion survey. After all, the environment and nature are very much "apple pie" issues; who could be against them (in part this is a rhetorical question, as the recent environmental backlash shows that many can oppose environmental identifications)? But many fewer people "act" environmentally.

Therefore, one dimension of environmentalism, in addition to thoughts about growth versus conservation, has to be activism, or the willingness to perform behaviors typically associated with environmentalism. This could range from very simple things like recycling to more involved commitments such as belonging to environmental groups to total absorption as in the case of radical environmentalists who order all aspects of their life according to environmental principles. Of course, we have already argued that such a lifestyle cannot be firmly based in scientific fact, although it can be grounded in the master-environmentalist story that would give it meaning.

The behavioral dimension of the environmental narrative is somewhat more difficult to judge and introduces a question of relativity into the environmental debate. For instance, a person who practiced recycling in the 1960s was a "committed" activist in the vanguard of radical conservationist practice. A person who recycles in the 1990s simply is conforming to local law or admitting the basic fact that landfill space is dwindling. Thus, standards for environmental practice change with time. To measure environmental behavior "absolutely" is not possible, so an examination of people's performance on this dimension has to be done relatively; that is, we should consider how environmentally concerned one's behavior is relative to basic social norms. Again, social norms can only be evaluated with respect to stories disseminated by dominant social and narrative elites. So even environmental "practice" must be judged against narrative criteria.

Still another dimension of the environmental narrative is that of political ideology. One normally assumes that environmentalism is a "liberal" trait, and indeed there is some evidence from opinion surveys showing substantial correlations between liberalism and environmentalism. Still, there is also a strong conservative branch of environmentalism, embodied by patrician land conservation groups, outdoors clubs, and environmental organizations focusing on traditional pursuits of the rich such as hunting and fishing. Environmentalists can make strange bedfellows on many occasions, and it might not be surprising to see a bearded antinuclearist make common cause with a fly-fishing stockbroker to protect a river from being dammed. One can add that many environmentalists come to environmentalism from a less ideological position. They simply "enjoy nature," and find that this enjoyment can become politicized as they find nature threatened. For this reason, environmentalism can tend to create its own ideological mass, as seen in the development of Green parties around the world, and in the fact that environmentalism is increasingly coming to appear on the issue agenda of many otherwise apolitical people. Environmental ideologies and narratives seem to have their own autonomous and wide appeal.

Still another dimension of the environmental narrative, related to the idea of political ideology, concerns the perception of collective versus individual action in the environmental arena. Some environmentalists strongly feel that collective governmental and societal action are required to effect environmental protection, whereas others feel that individually motivated action is required to generate truly global change. That also has to do with the sense of personal efficacy one has with regard to environmental matters. Thinking about personal efficacy, early media theorists developed the idea of *well-informed futility* (Wiebe, 1973), a concept in which the individual becomes "narcotized" by the onslaught of difficult-to-process information about environmental problems. Yet, many people have been strongly motivated to feel that their own individual action constitutes not only a contribution to environmental protection but also a powerfully communicative model for others to follow.

Beyond these narrative dimensions, environmentalism varies considerably by specific topics of concern. For instance, one person's concern over political issues related to development may oppose another's concern to protect marine species, or a third person's concern to abate noise pollution, or a fourth person's concern to stop nuclear power.

So one can see that the environmental story has many strands, with multiple possibilities for putting them together, and multiple ways that the stories can conflict. Environmentalism and the environment it represents are complex social constructs, gaining in complexity with time. Nowadays, in fact, the attractiveness of environmentalism as a "clean" political issue has meant that various political camps attempt to co-opt environmental terminology for their own use. The business community has certainly been active in this area; even explicitly anti-environmental groups, such as those belonging to the "wise use" movement, exploit environmentally tinged names for their purposes. Thus, examining environmentalism cleanly in today's communicative environment is becoming increasingly difficult. It is no longer possible to expect that the messages from this complex system will generate simple effects, if they ever did. An analysis is called for that can, to some extent, identify the main currents of media environmentalism and then specify effects according to such an analysis.

Table 1.1 presents a summary of some of the dimensions of environmentalism we have identified. Throughout the book we examine how media narratives have contributed to beliefs on these dimensions. Table 1.1 also includes some questions about narrative issues that could arise with respect to each dimension.

At this point we treat these narrative dimensions of environmental issues as open for question and investigation. But it also helps to have some overarching framework with which to investigate the relations between media presentation of the environment and people's narrative understandings of the environment. To do this we turn to the concept of the *dominant social paradigm* (DSP).

Recent scholarship on environmental sociology has identified a "paradigmatic" shift our environmental consciousness (e.g., Dunlap, 1992). According to these scholars' view we have entered an era in which our primary concern is neither economic progress nor technological development nor change for change's sake, but environmental preservation, stasis, diversity, and sustainability. We have made and are making the transition from a DSP of human-centered progress to a new environmental paradigm (NEP) of ecologically centered sustainability. Kempton Boster, and Hartley (1995) espoused this view, noting that many indicators of various kinds prove that "a substantial change is taking place in the way

Table 1.1. Dimensions of Environmentalism and Their Narrative Significance.

Dimension	Environmentalist Position	"Anti-environmentalist" Position	Narrative Issues
Growth vs. Stasis	Growth is not itself valuable, conservation and sustainability are preferred values	Growth represents progress	Do stories promote growth and consumerism? Is growth a moral focus of dominant narrative paradigm?
Anthropocentrism	Humans are one species among many, not the highest order	Humans are dominant species, with access to "resources"	How are nonhumans "characterized" in dominant narratives?
Intentionality	All entities that act purposively have rights	Only humans have rights	Who is portrayed as carrying out actions in dominant narratives?
Systems	Systems values of diversity, complexity, integrity, harmony, stability, and scarcity are valuable	Things have value according to standards set by humans	Do dominant narratives favor systems values or human-centered values?
Individual behavior	Environmentalists believe individual behavior contributes to collective good	Individuals act in their own best interest	Who acts in dominant narratives heroic individuals or communities?
Political Ideology	Environmentalists are typically liberal, although not exclusively	Anti-environmentalists are normally more conservative	Who tells stories in dominant narrative? What ideologies do they espouse?

Americans conceive of the environment" (p. 7). For these and other scholars, polling data about environmental concern, changes in purchasing habits, and political and policy trends are convincing evidence for the paradigm shift. In their view, the old paradigm emphasizing human dominion is being replaced by a new model stressing a wider and more diverse concept of environmental values and ethics, throwing in a new conception of humanity in the bargain.

But even given the agreement in civil discourse on the importance of the environment, it is probably too early to close the book on the DSP that today's environmentalist sees in his or her rear-view mirror. Objectively speaking, the social and economic world of 1995 was little different from the world of 1895, 1945, or even 1975. As far as daily life and "everyday" social reality were concerned, most people shared the same broad aims, most national economies were still growth-oriented, and the world was not much different in terms of the kinds of projects that societies and people seemed to choose for themselves. Although some studies asserted that people wanted to scale back or downsize their lives, booming stock markets and "right-sized" corporations highlighted that the bottom line was as important as it ever had been. Republican and even Democratic efforts to turn back important environmental legislation showed that hard-won environmental gains were not so easy to protect in the "new" paradigm. Thus, although our technological capacities increased manyfold since 1895—or even since 1975—we think that there has always been and still is one important foundational idea: "Progress" is an axiomatic good, and it can be achieved through technological genius, individual work, and motivation to profit. The continuing move toward a center-conservative and growth-oriented ideological position in U.S. politics can certainly be taken as evidence for this assertion. Indeed, the strength of the recent environmental "backlash" shows the continuing importance of the dominant growth paradigm (Easterbrook, 1995; Simon, 1995).

The evidence of our senses, supplied from today's media and popular culture, suggests that our environmental paradigm is changing, but these senses can also confuse. In our discourse, especially, we have become more accustomed to dealing with the environmental consequences of actions, and have learned to speak and act in ways which recognize that all things happen within a vaguely and sometimes ideologically defined environment. An "environmentally correct" discourse has emerged, even to the extent that some have proposed revising "species-ist" and "anti-natural" language (Ross, 1991). But despite this, one can argue that we have paid little attention, at the social level, to altering our basic lifeways, still seeking higher consumption, more comfort, more fun, and, in the end, "progress" toward a variety of goals.

Is this the new environmental paradigm? Kempton et al. (1995) cited phenomena such as discontinuance of aerosol spray can use as major evidence of the shift toward environmentalism. If we conceive of environmentalism as a bandage on the perceived wounds of industrialism, clearly we have made major progress. Recycling certainly is better than waste disposal without recycling, and other lifestyle shifts portend an incremental move toward more rational resource consumption, but is it evidence for a paradigmatic shift?

As a graduate student pointed out recently, people tend to overuse the word *paradigm* these days. We may be well advised to let future generations mark our age as the watershed for a new environmental paradigm. Those who say we are experiencing a paradigmatic shift may mean that our perception of the world, the universe, and the environment have subtly changed, such that "The Environment" is foregrounded more often in a variety of discussions (although we see that even this assertion is debatable). But in a true paradigm shift, we would expect our conception of the environment to change, and our position in relation to it. This conceptual shift would produce behavior changes much unlike anything we have currently seen, including a radical downsizing of social structures, major values changes, and massive political restructuring. Indeed, it may well be impossible to know whether the social-environmental paradigm has shifted because the proper sense of the term indicates that one cannot understand what a new paradigm looks like until one has emerged into it (Kuhn, 1962). Taking this more conservative view of recent environmental attitude changes, one is tempted to argue that any attitudinal or opinion shifts that have actually taken place should be seen as occurring within the still-dominant Western social paradigm. Perceptual shifts occurring within the paradigm are communication phenomena, above all, and are one of the important aspects of environmental thinking dealt with in this book. Indeed, in this book we argue that the institutions of the mass media serve an important paradigm-maintenance function. We ask the reader to assume with us at this point that paradigm change has been overhyped; in later chapters, we provide data that bear on the issue.

WHAT "IS" AN ENVIRONMENTALIST?

All of these questions (paradigms, narrative, dimensions of environmentalism, etc.) are important to individuals as they construct their own thinking about the environment. But within the current social paradigm, we also have to accept that some decisions are not up to individuals. Anyone who obeys the basic ground rules of modern life accepts, often unquestioningly, that the environment is essentially a resource that funds human progress. One cannot exist in our society without making and accepting decisions that massively violate a so-called environmental ethic, because our "everyday" social reality assumes that the environment is a "resource." As Berger and Luckmann (1966) pointed out, one can question everyday reality only at the expense of enormous effort. "While I am capable of engaging in doubt about its reality, I am obliged to suspend such doubt as I routinely exist in everyday life" (p. 23). This raises a fundamental question, then. Can one "really" be an environmentalist in a society governed by an essentially anti-environmental paradigm?

If you answer "no" to this question, then you will probably also agree that to try to "be" an environmentalist is to live in a contradictory state with everyday social reality. This means that the environmentalist must engage in cognitive dissonance-reducing activities that lessen the contradictory condition. Because there is little hope of living up to the standards of the new environmental ethic in a material sense, the environmentalist must often turn his or her attention to the "symbolic" sphere where realities can be more easily manufactured and maintained.

For instance, a single trip on an airplane massively violates many of the environmental principles routinely discussed in most systems of environmental ethics. Remembering that an absolute majority of U.S. citizens claim to be environmentalists,[2] it is not absurd to assert that today's "average" environmentalist is just as likely to be concerned about the recyclability of the soda can he or she might use on that flight (an issue over which a person can assert some control), while letting the question of massive air pollution as a result of the flight go unanswered or simply ignored. At one level, this is a massive contradiction. At another, however, it is freely accepted. Why? Such a paradox is a result of the fact that a communicational environment tends to stand in for the "real" one in the minds of many. In the communicational environment, the recyclability of the soda can is an important "environmental" decision that consumers can make while airplanes are simply an unquestioned mode of travel in everyday social reality.

This is not to question the motives of environmentalists who have effected many improvements in modern living. Our discussion

---

[2]For instance, the percentage of respondents in the 1993 General Social Survey who thought the United States was spending "too little" on problems of the environment was 55.7. In 1994 the percentage was 58.8.

simply points out that communication and symbolism play enormous roles in today's environmentalism. But communication asserts more than a reflective role; it also has a constitutive role in environmental problems. Precisely because communication can construct environments it is so important to an understanding of "the" environment (i.e., the natural world). For the average environmentalist, the complexity of making judgments about the environment must often be put on the back burner when deciding what is environmentally correct, with ideological and perhaps even symbolically constructed concerns playing just as important a role as, say, scientific facts. Most people "see" recycling as an "environmental" decision, whereas airplanes are simply a way to get to the next environmental conference. Indeed, if a "paradigm" is what helps us see certain things and not see others (as Kuhn argued), one must question whether the new environmental paradigm has been very successful at all or has merely introduced new ways to talk about the environment.

As we investigate the contributions of media to our environmental understandings, we want to keep in mind that "environmental" decisions are made by people often using narrative criteria. This means that stories and images ("narrative rationality") rather than facts and scientific arguments ("technical rationality") help to determine what we think we know about the environment. By extension, in a process first discussed by Lippmann (1922), these stories and images may come to stand in as environment.

PERSPECTIVES ON ENVIRONMENTAL DISCOURSE

None of this means that the environment "goes away." Stories do not excise reality. But we do see a narrative struggle going on. That is, the dominant social paradigm requires narrative work to help rationalize its uneasy coexistence with the real environment. The media institutions we examine have important roles to play in this struggle (we argue that they play an essentially conservative and sometimes reactionary role).

Berry (1988) agreed that environmentalism is about stories, although he sees the dominant Western narrative as mostly deficient. He said "We are in trouble just now because we do not have a good story. We are in between stories. The old story, the account of how the world came to be and how we fit into it, is no longer effective. Yet we have not learned the new story" (p. 123). This is also our analysis, although we see a narrative struggle rather than a passive transitional period. Although Berry viewed perhaps an organic transition from the dominant narrative paradigm (DNP; a term that might replace DSP), we argue that cultural institutions and socioeconomic elites benefit from the current narrative perspective. Because elites benefit from the DNP, they tend to attempt to enforce its reception. Although the environmental poverty of the current narrative paradigm may be evident to scholars such as Berry, the DNP continues to dominate the commercial systems for disseminating stories, and by extension is very influential in the mass communication of environmental issues.

If the problems of today's environmental narratives are seen as reflecting objective environmental and systemic contradictions (as Berry and others might argue), then the appearance of an environmental narrative crisis in recent years makes theoretical sense. But it is difficult to imagine that the dominant social and narrative paradigms, serving economic interests as they do, can go down without a fight. So today's environmentalism, as understood by the mass public, is not just the output of committed activists who are out to change the world. It is about a narrative struggle to both frame and claim a reworked concept of nature. As we see here, narrative contests can become messy. Although the committed environmentalist harbors a particular vision of environmental progress, the dominant media systems are busy co-opting and reclaiming that vision so that it fits within a more mainstream conception of how the world should work. This narrative struggle is contested on an uneven pitch: The field is tilted strongly toward the narrative "elites." An important aim of this book is to study the output of the narrative elites who work through the mass media, and to determine how their messages are received.

OUTLINE OF THE BOOK

This volume focuses on narrative and the environment. In this introductory chapter, we have sketched a brief understanding of today's environmental issues and why they should be studied from a narrative perspective. The overall aim of the book is to examine the role of mass media, especially television, in the construction of the environment from a dominant narrative perspective.

Chapter 2 looks more deeply at theory and research in the area of media and the environment. We start with some theory relevant to the social construction of the environment. Then we examine specific studies that have examined media's role in constructing environmental knowledge, beliefs, attitudes, and behavior. This very in-depth account shows that scholars are slowly but inexorably beginning to understand that stories play a very important role in people's understanding of their own environment.

Chapter 3 looks more specifically at the issue of narrative. We introduce ideas from the literature on narrative to complement our understanding of media's role. In this chapter, we explain how media research, combined with a narrative understanding, can provide a useful way to examine today's environmental issues.

In Chapter 4, we look at television's characterization of the environment. In particular, we focus on the role played by prime-time television, an area that has been poorly studied in relation to environmental stories. Because television programs are an essential feature of the dominant narrative paradigm, we argue that their messages about the environment can give important clues to an understanding of today's environmental problems.

In Chapter 5, we examine "effects" from television's messages about the environment. Using cultivation analysis, we explore relationships between individuals' attention to television and their beliefs and knowledge about environmental issues.

In Chapter 6, we examine how journalism deals with environmental issues. In particular, we focus on the issue of global warming. We argue that the prevalence of "cycles" in attention to environmental issues is really a feature of the dominant narrative paradigm that requires that issues be interesting and motivate audience attention.

Finally, we attempt to put these pieces together into a coherent narrative about environmental narrative: a meta-story, if you will. We consider the future directions in which environmental narrative seems to be heading and propose directions for further research to abet understanding.

two

PREVIOUS RESEARCH ON THE MEDIATED ENVIRONMENT

THE "SOCIAL" ENVIRONMENT

The idea of a *social environment* is certainly not new and can be understood in several ways. One use of the term *environment* is potentially misleading, because the word is often used simply to indicate a "milieu" or "context." That is not the use we intend to make of the term here, although the social context is undoubtedly intertwined with the social environment as we understand it. Simply, the social environment is the social conception that every culture makes of its environment.

Evernden (1992) gave perhaps the most interesting and full treatment of the social environment in *The Social Creation of Nature*. Some communication theorists are beginning to apply constructionist ideas to the environment, leading to studies such as Hansen's (1991) "The Media and the Social Construction of the Environment." This chapter reviews these ideas, examines some of the relevant problems these studies raise for media effects research, and further defines the theory of the social environment. We then examine studies that have looked at the nature and impacts of media "information" on environmental beliefs and attitudes.

Evernden did not specifically implicate media in his research on social conceptions of the environment, although the connection is transparent. Evernden's idea is quite simple but important:

> there *is* a metaphysic lying behind the simple existence of the word *nature*. It is not simply a description of a found object: it is also an assertion of a relationship. Furthermore, it plays a role . . . in the daily life of a society through the social use we make of it. If there is nature, one can speak of things belonging to nature, or of being "natural." And if there are things that are natural, one can also speak of others as "unnatural." In the earlier use of nature as everything that is, this would not be possible. But if there can be something else, if nature is not everything, then some things may exist that are either beyond nature or *against* nature. (p. 21; emphasis in original)

In this view, *nature* itself is partly a communication or language decision about what counts as *natural.* It is the invention of a word, at least, with all the implications attendant thereto. Evernden's historical conception of nature as a changing, culturally dependent construct, tied to but independent of physical reality, suggests that this notion of environment can be subsumed within the general debate on the *social construction of reality.* This phrase can perhaps be seen as the center of gravity of all current debate in social theory, so it is not unlikely that the environment and its conceptions should come to be discussed as part of this problem.

The idea of the social construction of reality is one of the most charged and potentially misunderstood concepts in the recent social theory discourse. The term is often used by those who wish to argue that there is no such thing as reality, that objective facts do not exist, and that value systems are always and necessarily completely contingent, as opposed to invariant or based on some foundational truth. This certainly does not seem to have been the intention of Berger and Luckmann (1966), who wrote the most well-known work on the subject, *The Social Construction of Reality.* Their view of social reality does not deny that other realities exist. Simply, the concept of *social reality* was designed as a response to sociologies not sufficiently grounded in day-to-day reality and, therefore, not reflective of real-life problems. Social reality is simply the set of practices and understandings of everyday life that guide people in their actions.

However, with regard to the environment, there are two important points to make. First, having a social idea of nature does not deny the existence of a "real" environment. As we have already said, this real environment is sufficiently complex that we cannot completely know it, but it does exist. Second, the relationship between the social construction of the environment and its real natural state is a key problem today. It is precisely the "ultimately" absolute state of the environment that makes our more relative conception problematic. As Evernden (1992) concluded, "if we would protect nature from the perils of the 'environmental crisis,' we must first acknowledge that those perils arose as a consequence of conceptual imprisonment" (p. 130).

A slightly more conservative approach to the idea of the social environment simply suggests that "information" is a natural component of any environment—sometimes described as the "symbolic environment." As early as 1980, Ploman argued:

> As the concept of environment is now used it encompasses not only the physical environment, including all man-made features, but also the social environment, which includes the symbolic environment and the communications/information complex; the physical sphere, the biosphere, and the noosphere. It would therefore be perfectly logical to consider the information environment of individuals and groups as corresponding to the communications ecology of societies. This approach would be valuable in that our understanding of the environment seems at least some steps ahead of our thinking about communications. The concept of information as symbolic environment not separate from but part of the wider environment might even help us better to tackle the complex interrelationship between both of them. (p. 22)

Also, the term *constructionism* has been used fairly often in recent communication research, mostly as a way of rejecting earlier notions of media "effects." Hansen (1991) took this approach in his "constructionist" view of environmental communication. One common criticism of media effects research is that it designs itself so as to find what it is intended to find.

> Because their starting point is a search for media *influence* on public opinion, this is essentially what they end up finding. And in this respect they repeat a transmission view, in which it is assumed that environmental meanings flow from certain sources through the media to the wider public. (p.446)

Actually, given that it is true that many effects studies are "artificially" designed to find effects, it is surprising that relatively few of them do find strong effects. At least in the environmental area, effects research has not conclusively shown that media are major determinants of environmentalism, either in terms of belief or attitude. Still, Hansen's idea that the environment is especially subject to constructionist phenomena is an important one. Rather than searching for direct influences of media variables, then, we might also follow Hansen's lead in searching for "cultural resonances" in the production of environmental meanings. Such cultural resonances would be evidence of the larger social scheme in which media operate. We think that Hansen's attempt to get away from traditional media effects research actually offers us a way to recast effects studies in a more culturally realistic way.

As an attempt to clear up the lexicon somewhat, let us define three terms: the *social environment*, the social *construction* of the environment, and the *natural* environment. The middle term is easiest: The social construction of the environment is a predominantly held conception of the natural world, including relatively cognitive attitudes, beliefs, and behaviors relevant to the environment. The social environment is the socially latent but deeply important cultural definition of what is "environmental." As such, it is a deeper, more unconscious, and unquestioned set of assumptions and beliefs about nature. This set of assumptions may be encoded even at the linguistic level, which makes it difficult to analyze. The natural environment is the actual, physical environment and the objectively real physical relationships that persist in that system.

One might say that these terms exist at three separate levels, each characterized by relatively lesser systematic complexity. The natural environment is the "ground" on which all environmental communication must eventually achieve meaning. Note that we say "eventually," because we have already argued that social constructions of the environment need not correspond in any direct way to the experienced physical environment. We merely mean that the natural environment exerts pressures on social constructions that must be accounted for at some point. The complexity of the natural system is relatively high because it is the system that encompasses all others. The social environment is derived partially from this system, although at a level in which individual human cognition is relatively meaningless. The social environment is similar to the "objectification" idea proposed by Berger and Luckmann (1996), in which successive generations of humans lay down foundations of meaning. Newly born individuals encounter these objectifications as objective facts, although they were socially constructed at one time and are subject to change. One might also think of the social environment as a *paradigm*, a term used by many (as we have seen) in discussing the change of ideas of nature and environment. Our description indicates that a social environment, or paradigm, is relatively resistant to change. Finally, built on the previous two, is the social construction of the environment, which is essentially the current thinking about environmental issues at the level at which one can identify specific ideas and "opinions." These "constructions" may be identified as environmental perceptions, beliefs, attitudes, and so on.

This means that relatively ephemeral notions of the environment ("current events" or "public opinion") are formed within the context of a relatively less ephemeral social notion of environment, handed down to us from our cultural forebears. This superstructure sits, either easily or uneasily, on the physical "fact" of the natural environment.

All three aspects of the environment are of interest here. Social constructions of the environment stand to be influenced by media portrayals in obvious and direct ways. Ideas, facts, and images about the environment are supplied from the media on a daily basis. Undoubtedly, many of the "concerns" we think of as relating to the environment are supplied from media reports and portrayals. Thus, an important research question is how the media "portray" the environment, and how they affect social "construction."

At the next deeper level, however, it may be that media portrayals and images reflect deeper ideological commitments about the environment. If so, these would be harder to detect because they would exist at the level of the social objectification. Yet, if we are to be interested in the impacts of communication systems on environmental ideologies, it is also at the level of the social environment that we must look. Thus, there may be deeper ideological effects that we wish to hypothesize. In particular, discussions of any relationships between media messages and a "new environmental paradigm" must be conducted at the level of the social environment.

At the deepest level there is mystery. Do our systems of representing the environment have effects on the environment itself? In a simple sense they certainly do, if we can agree that our knowledge and images either cause us or prevent us from engaging in actions that might preserve or conserve. But at a deeper level, whether our systems of communication can be brought into a more stable relationship with the natural environment is a question that begs research and an answer. We hope that the studies reported in this volume can begin to show the path to this kind of answer.

Next, we turn our attention to a summary of research results about media impacts on the environment. Most studies operate at the shallowest level: media's impact on what we call the social *construction* of the environment. However, some researchers have begun the more difficult task of penetrating to the ideological issue, with implications even for the deepest question: Do media representations influence the natural environment?

MEDIA AND THE ENVIRONMENT

In today's world, the narrative function is largely subsumed by the mass media. If we are to give an account of today's nature stories, we must look at mass communication, the unquestioned dominant purveyor of today's mythologies.

In media effects research, the questions of greatest interest have been: How powerful are media messages? How powerfully do media shape attitudes? Do messages affect behavior? Do they modify and change opinions? All these questions are relevant to environmentalism. In some ways, the environment represents a perfect candidate for potential media change. It is a problem of relevance to all, there has been widespread apathy, yet part of the problem is simply one of constructing attitude and linking it to action. Although there are ways to think about media other than an effects approach, most of the literature on media and the environment has emerged from this perspective.

In the area of the environment, there have been three major categories of media research. The first has simply to do with content, trying to find out how the media portray the environment. Mostly, these studies use content analyses to depict and trace the nature of environmental content, in order to provide a sense of just how well the media are doing their "job" of covering this issue. More rarely, such content analyses are used to develop a more sophisticated analysis about what the media "should" be doing. In any case, most of these studies focus on news portrayals, with the lion's share of these devoted to print research, due to the relative ease of collecting print stories for analysis. Broadcast media have been less analyzed in this category.

The second category concerns the effects of various media in the area of the environment. This research is somewhat more diverse than the content research. Any study attempting to measure or assess an outcome of particular media messages or systems of messages can be considered an effects study. Many studies have focused on the effects of single messages or single environmental campaigns. Because these kinds of studies are considered practical, they have received some research funding over the years; environmental communication studies, along with agricultural communication, rural sociology, and research on the diffusion of innovations, have all provided a general framework for approaching environmental problems as a cognitive-level issue solvable with specific messages. Within this category, a second group of studies has examined journalistic portrayals of the environment and their effects, again with a heavy concentration on print.

The third category of research, more loosely categorized as media effects research, concerns environmental ideology and its relationship to the media and culture. This research, drawing broadly from a critical approach to culture, has not provided pragmatic approaches to solving environmental problems but has clearly raised the level of sophistication in environmental debate. Among all kinds of research, these studies tend to account for broadcast forms of media more frequently, although without data-driven tests of hypotheses. We now examine research from each of these areas in some detail.

CONTENT RESEARCH

In reviewing media effects research, we limit ourselves to a post-1960's analysis. A few studies may exist prior to this period, but the bulk of media research on the question was motivated by the appearance of the environment as a social issue in the late 60s.

Many of the earliest studies simply described the appearance of the environment as an issue in the media. Funkhouser (1973) examined coverage of 1960's issues through an analysis of *Reader's Guide* citations. He noted that coverage of pollution and ecology was particularly heavy in 1970 as a result of the inaugural Earth Day. *Ecology* (later environmentalism) was considered to be more important as a public opinion issue in years in which it was more heavily covered.

Although the environment was a hot issue in the 1970s, we should not assume that it dominated the issue agenda. Schoenfeld (1979) found that environmentalism is one of many issues whose agenda may often be set by factors other than the media. In the case of the Environmental Protection Agency enabling legislation (NEPA), Schoenfeld concluded that, even though the 1970s were a period of public environmental concern, actual coverage of the EPA legislating process was slight, with the agenda being set by Congress rather than by the media.

Althoff, Greig, and Stuckey (1973) examined environmental attitudes of media managers in Kansas to depict the general receptiveness toward environmental problems at a crucial time in the development of environmentalism. They determined that media gatekeepers at the local level had not internalized an environmental ethic, even though the early 1970's was a time of significant environmental concern. Editors listed the environment as last on a series of problems of concern. Because various media were tied to advertising from known polluters, managers' opinions about the environment were somewhat diluted. The authors concluded that local readers received an unrealistic view of environmental problems due to these factors.

Clearly, however, the 1970's were an important decade for a focus on "ecology" and environmental problems. Bowman and Hanaford (1977) examined coverage of the issue in mass market magazines in the period 1971 to 1975. Some mass market periodicals, such as *Reader's Digest*, printed numerous articles on environmental issues or problems. Other magazines selected as controls, such as *Better Homes and Gardens*, published fewer articles. Although coverage of environmental problems was sporadically prominent (a pattern that continues to the 1990's), environmentalism did not overwhelm magazines where one would not expect it, and even where one would expect it, such as *National Geographic*.

Bowman and Fuchs (1981) also examined magazine coverage of the environment over a two-decade period. They concluded that readers of some mass interest magazines were exposed to increasing coverage of environmental issues through the 1960's and 1970's. However, their study was extremely impressionistic and not conclusive, even though the data support the common sense impression that environmental coverage has increased over those decades.

Obviously, specific events influence media coverage of environmental events. As media research moved through the 1970s into the 1980's, a variety of more specialized and topic-oriented content analyses emerged. For instance, Nimmo and Combs (1982) analyzed TV coverage of the Three Mile Island incident. They emphasized differences in coverage by individual networks, in contrast to many media studies that treat news as an institutional bloc. They argued these differences are due to institutional "ethos." "Melodrama" was a key feature of the story, as in many environmental stories requiring dramatic events to motivate the coverage.

Many other studies have examined environmental portrayals from a scientific or "risk" perspective. These studies normally focus on how issues are presented and whether they meet a standard that one would expect for public understanding of scientific issues. For instance, Sullivan (1985) found that the press covered a food irradiation proposal extremely inadequately. Comparing press accounts to the "facts" of an FDA publication, he noted that most accounts were incomplete or inaccurate. Thus, he concluded the public could not be expected to adequately understand food irradiation.

Gale (1987) studied the portrayal of environmental risk in the case of Chernobyl. He noted that nuclear energy is a special kind of risk because it is perceived as an "imposed" risk, even though statistically the chances of being injured by nuclear energy are quite small compared to other risks. Therefore, news coverage of such environmental risks may tend to acquire an especially ominous character, regardless of the actual level of threat.

Friedman, Gorney, and Egolf (1987) also looked at Chernobyl coverage. Of primary interest in their study was coverage of radiation issues. As a prime environmental and health threat, it would be important for viewers to know exact information about radiation releases and to be able to make comparisons. Because the U.S. government had used Three Mile Island as a case study to create standards for coverage of radiation, Chernobyl could be held up to those standards. They found that the press skimped on radiation information, but that information provided was reasonable and fair.

Gorney (1992) found that TV portrayals of Chernobyl were sensationalized, dramatized, and exaggerated, producing a distortion of perception of the news value of the story and the risks involved. She concluded that viewers were not presented enough information to make adequate risk judgments. In general, Chernobyl was seen as a dramatic story by definition, and we should probably expect the subtler environmental aspects of such a story to be overshadowed.

The issue of environmental risk received increasing attention through the 1980's and into the 1990's. In their work, Krimsky and Plough (1988) argued that there are really two types of risk communication, conventional and symbolic. The difference between the two amounts to the difference between factual and image-based communication. Conventional risk communication informs people about risks. Symbolic risk communication develops stories about risks and ties them into cultural and social roles performed by actors involved in a risk event. In the media, as one would surmise, symbolic risk communication is extremely important: "The media places [sic] the issue of a risk event in bold relief; simplification, dramatization, and polarization are common, whereas inaccuracy and explicit bias are rare" (p. 299).

Singer and Endreny (1987) found that media emphasize harms rather than risks in news portrayals. The importance given to news stories is not related to the actual physical damage that may potentially be caused by a risk; rather, it is associated with factors related to the kind of risk involved. The more rare the risk, in many cases, the greater the frequency of portrayal in news media. Environmental dangers do not often conform to this schema.

Singer (1990) examined the way journalists deal with hazards in the news. She found that many scientific studies are
improperly reported in the news, although newspapers seem to do
a better job than radio and television. She noted:

> we can speculate that in the popular press science, and scien-
> tists, come across as more authoritative than they really are;
> that scientific findings are regarded with more confidence than
> may be warranted; that therefore, when a disconfirming finding
> comes along, it may undermine the credibility of the whole
> structure; and that confidence in the press, as well as in sci-
> ence, may suffer as a result. (p. 115)

Wilkins and Patterson (1991) studied the general presentation of risk, as well. They concluded that journalists are laypersons
when it comes to scientific subject matter, so journalists' own perceptions of risk are important in how they cover stories. They particularly noted the importance of symbols in covering risk. Stories
that acquire symbolic significance have a better chance of getting
covered; there is a symbolic "threshold" that stories need to reach
to get wide coverage. Their study of "greenhouse" coverage in 1987-
1988 found that the story did not reach such a symbolic threshold.
Other issues such as acid rain have attracted significant
research attention. Barton (1988) examined coverage of TV news of
acid rain and discussed some implications for Canadian-American
policy. As in other studies, conflict and drama of news presentations of environmental issues were highlighted. The story exists to
serve the purpose of the journalist rather than policy makers; thus,
narrative aspects are emphasized over substantive ones. Greenberg
Sachsman, Sandman, and Salamone (1989) found the same phenomenon, in that media are more influenced by the dramatic value
of a story than by the actual inherent risk in a story. Thus, very
risky phenomena might well be ignored if there were no particular
dramatic reason for presenting a story. Environmental news, like
all news, is subject to the same considerations any potential news
story is given. However, environmental news is particularly different from most stories because environmental problems tend to be
ongoing in nature.
Global warming studies appeared not long after the insur-
gence of public concern about the issue in the late 1980s. Kempton
(1991; Kempton et al., 1995) noted that the public tends to harbor
certain misunderstandings about global warming, particularly
because they connect the issue with previously held understandings and misunderstandings about the pollution issue. These "lay
perspectives" condition people's beliefs about global warming and

also condition the way people tend to perceive new information about the problem. Kempton noted that

> The problem of the public understanding of global climate change would probably work itself out over many years through science education in schools and media coverage. This process would be accelerated greatly if those who communicate with the public . . . specifically target some of the gaps and misleading prior models. (p. 207)

But other studies show that the media may also contribute to false and/or misleading information.

Bell (1994), for instance, reported that a significant minority of stories he examined contained errors or "misreporting" about global climate change. Although many of the errors were ones of omission or misquotation or poorly placed emphasis, taken together they imply that readers, even of "quality" newspapers, are likely to receive information that is considered incorrect by the scientific sources themselves.

Yet Wilkins' (1993) argument about global warming coverage is that the mass media are too focused on the science, without connecting the environmental issues to underlying values that need to be discussed. Because the greenhouse effect results from lifestyle and value choices, stories about the issue should reflect both aspects. But in Wilkins' view, print media coverage between 1987 and 1990 tended to focus on the "wrong" value, including the competitive aspects of climate change science and the "institutionalization" of knowledge in science and government. As is seen later, lifestyle values and environmental issues are often disconnected in media discourse.

Apart from risk and issue-oriented papers, studies appearing since the mid 1980's to late 1980's have been able to get some perspective on changes and patterns in the coverage of the environment in the media. For instance, Howenstine (1987) reported that environmental news stories from 1970-1982 increasingly focused on the integration of environmental problems within the rubric of the economic system, rather than presenting them as independent threats to such a system.

Fortner and Wiggington (1989) studied natural history programming on television, testing the idea that natural history programming declined over the period from 1973 to 1986. Although popular opinion was that wildlife and natural history programs had disappeared from the airwaves, there was in fact a significant increase noted in programming, although relatively fewer new productions were being made. Many of the new programs, incidentally, appeared on cable.

Patterson and Wilkins (1990) examined coverage of "slow-onset" environmental problems (problems of an ongoing nature) and found they were generally covered as "quick-onset" events. Very few of such stories had a scientific focus, with most of them taking a specific news "peg" as the reason for coverage. This is true of almost all environmental coverage. The authors pointed out that "Hardly mentioned was the fact that most of the elusive hazards are a product of a lifestyle that includes high mobility, comfortable air-conditioning, and other benefits of technology" (p. 18).

McKibben (1992) watched all programming recorded from a Virginia cable system on a day in May and then compared the experience of watching the shows and advertisements to spending a day in the Adirondacks. He argued that television programming detracts from our awareness of the environment, replacing it with new knowledge of a different type. To McKibben, this explains why we exist in an "age of missing information."

Shanahan (1996) examined prime-time television programming in 1991 and 1993 to determine the frequency of appearance of environmental messages and the context within which viewers would be expected to encounter such messages. Environmental messages were found to be few and far between. Nature and environmental themes are sporadic within the context of a greater focus on themes such as sex, crime, family, relationships, as so forth. These data are examined more closely in chapter 4.

Cottle (1993) discussed the general patterns of presentation of environmental news in Britain, with implications for U.S. news. He noted, first of all, that environmental news is relatively rare, amounting to about 4% of all news stories. Of these, pollution stories and stories about wildlife are the most common, perhaps because of their visual appeal. Environmental politics was underemphasized. Testing Hall, Crichter, Jefferson, Clarke, and Roberts' (1978) notion of "primary definers," he found that news identifies several kinds of groups as legitimate authorities on environmental issues. In fact, environmental pressure groups gained the most opportunity to speak about environmental issues, partly because the news stories were often generated by their own public relations apparatus. Most importantly, environmental issues are almost always seen in a particular way to be made meaningful to the "home viewer":

> Whether concerned with Green tourism, the growth of sales in mineral waters, the impact of global warming on British holiday weather, or 'body ecology', the environment becomes refracted through a journalistic prism frequently seeking to appeal to the immediate domestic and leisure concerns of ordinary consumers. (Cottle, 1993, p. 128)

The need to bend stories to fit the dominant narrative paradigm is evidenced.

Einsiedel and Coughlan (1993) examined coverage of environment in the Canadian press. Their analysis confirms the widespread perception that environmental coverage increased in the late 1980's. More interestingly, they noted that many of the stories they covered tended to adopt a more holistic tone, linking what had previously been seen as separate problems. Also, environmental coverage increasingly began to display a cyclical nature: First acid rain dominated the stage (at least in Canada where it was a prime political hot potato), then ozone, then global warming, followed by tropical rain forest issues. Except for acid rain, most of these issues had about a 5-year life cycle.

A variety of case studies presented descriptions of how journalists cover environmental issues. Dunwoody and Griffin (1993) found that two important factors tend to determine coverage of environmental issues in newspapers. One is the framework journalists typically use in constructing stories. Personal "schemata" of journalists tend to frame stories based on the routines of news practice, and the conventions of narrative. The second factor concerns the local political context, which can be either pluralistic or nonpluralistic. Pluralistic communities emphasize conflict in their local news coverage, whereas smaller, more homogeneous communities take a consensus approach. In their analysis of coverage of Superfund sites, the authors found that newspapers relied to a great extent on the EPA construction of the story and that news sources in the story exercised a great deal of control over the portrayal of important issues. Also, news coverage in smaller communities confined coverage to specific events, in an attempt to "contain" the issue and minimize threats to established political order. This practice was less likely in more heterogeneous communities with more confrontational press systems. Neither system escapes the conventions of journalistic practice, however.

Salamone, Greenberg, Sandman, and Sachsman (1990) presented interesting data on how various "actors" in environmental reporting tend to perceive and evaluate environmental stories. They found that journalists tend to place less emphasis on scientific accuracy in their evaluations than other actors such as scientists, government officials, or activists. Journalists apparently use a constellation of factors to judge whether an environmental story is excellent. The presence of risk information, along with alarming imagery, was more important to journalists. These findings confirm somewhat the notion that journalists look for good stories instead of pure facts.

Wilkins (1990) also addressed the important issue of how journalists should cover issues such as the environment. Environmental coverage can be problematic if reporters somehow succumb to the temptation to become "advocates" for a position instead of being objective reporters of environmental problems. Wilkins particularly identified the problem of reporting on "future" issues. Many environmental problems are problems that may emerge in the future, yet the mass media are much more geared to presenting events that occur "in the now." Wilkins argued that democratic ethics require that the mass media, performing a politically democratic function, ideally should adopt a somewhat more future-oriented perspective.

> What is required is that journalists articulate clearly for both themselves and their readers and viewers that one of the responsibilities of a late 20th century press in a democracy is to take news about the future—and the policy options that will produce it—seriously. (p.100)

The advocacy vs. objectivity issue was also explored in LaMay and Dennis' (1991) book, *Media and the Environment* (1991).

Hansen's (1993a) study of Greenpeace is an example of the kind of content research that can go beyond simple counting of stories and themes. He found that Greenpeace, in Britain, is notable not only for the amount of coverage it receives, but also for the particular way in which it achieves status as a claims-making entity. Hansen noted that in some years, environmental group action and environmental group claims-making constitute the largest categories of environmental stories, with even the government trailing as a source. Given this, it is rather important to understand the particular political character of an organization. For some issues, coverage and public concern can be seen almost entirely as a function of Greenpeace public communication activity; in other cases, despite Greenpeace promotions, coverage is relatively independent. An implication of Hansen's overall argument is that numerical patterns of coverage may obscure interesting facts that can only be found at the level of the individual story.

It is difficult to generalize about the enormous variety of studies on environmental mass communication content. However, one consistently emerging theme relates to narrative. Environmental mass communication is hardly ever the simple communication of a "fact"; what scientists may perceive as the misreporting and misunderstanding of scientific data and results can be seen as a natural outcome of audiences' tendencies to use narrative structures for processing information. Similarly, journalists use narrative structures to build interesting environmental coverage. The studies on environmental communication show that media portrayals of environmental issues are presented from the start as stories; because journalists and media programmers must interest audiences, they must present their information in narrative packages. Whether we use terms such as *symbolic, narrative,* or *sensational* to describe qualities of environmental communication, research reveals that mediated attempts to talk about the environment consistently depart from simple information and reporting.

Media content research has many separate strands, ranging from simple descriptive statistical work to more complex qualitative casc studies. Most of these studies point to the need, however, for work in the effects area to understand how these complex content patterns are internalized by mass media audiences. Although there is less work in the effects area, enough exists to begin seeing the boundaries of the impacts of the content described previously.

Effects Research

As noted earlier, effects research is any research that measures or assesses an outcome from audience exposure to media content. Many effects studies note rather weak outcomes; often, the outcomes are considered "correlates" of the media content with which they are associated. That is, some studies do not make direct links between exposure and content (e.g., studies that compare public opinion shifts to broad-scale media shifts). Other studies examine direct connections between specific programs and specific outcomes, such as increases in knowledge due to media campaigns or documentaries. These studies' heritage is found in the classic research on media effects (Bryant & Zillmann 1994), as well as in the tradition of agricultural extension research that seeks to increase direct effectiveness of media messages. Some other studies simply examine public opinion states and infer media messages from those states.

A variety of theories and hypotheses abounds in the media effects field. Most of these theories have been tested with environmental issues. For instance, Bailey (1970) found that increased coverage of the environment validated the "knowledge gap" hypothesis. That is, higher socioeconomic status (SES) consumers of news increase their knowledge of the environment at a faster rate than those lower on the SES ladder. This is explained by environmentalism being primarily a phenomenon of the upper classes, and mass communication information being more effective when actively sought out by audiences.

An early study by Novic and Sandman (1974) raised important questions. They studied relationships between mass media use
and attitudes toward solutions for environmental problems.
Contrary to commonsense, heavy users of mass media were less
informed, viewed environmental problems less seriously, and preferred less "personal" solutions to environmental problems. The
authors argued:

> If mass media use results in less personal commitment to envi-
> ronmental improvement than use of non-mass sources, then it
> is important to ask what characteristics of the media are
> responsible for the difference. If, on the other hand, environ-
> mental commitment results in a change from mass to nonmass
> information sources, then it is important to examine the role of
> mass media in spurring or impeding the growth of that commit-
> ment. (p. 42)

These comments delineated the basic problem for media
effects research about contributions to the construction of social
reality. Should media be seen as causes or symptoms of environmental concern? Novic and Sandman suggested that one should
not examine media as either cause or effect, but as a reciprocal
cause and effect, entwined in a social feedback system where opinions are not only generated by media coverage but reinforced by
media coverage and recruitment from the ranks of previously
unconvinced public opinion.

Like Novic and Sandman, Ostman and Parker (1987)
explored basic correlations between demographic variables and
media use with environmental knowledge and behaviors. In particular, they underlined an expected negative relation between age
and environmentalism and a positive relation between education
and environmentalism. More interestingly, confirming Novic and
Sandman's findings, they also noted a negative relationship with
television use and environmentalism.

One of the major conclusions of media research is that
mediated information campaigns are less "powerful" than interpersonal forms of communication in producing behavior change (Rice
& Atkin, 1994). This finding is particularly prominent in the area of
the environment. For instance, former President Jimmy Carter
offered media theorists a natural experiment in media effectiveness
when he undertook to decrease energy consumption in a series of
public campaigns during the U.S. energy crisis in 1970 (he termed
the problem the *moral equivalent of war*). Allen and Weber (1983)
found that these efforts, covered widely in all media, were largely
ineffectual.

Perceptions of change in consumption and general feelings of effectiveness were not influenced by Energy Week. Such perceptions and feelings have been linked to locus of control and may be highly resistant to change as a result." (p. 104)

Locus of control is the technical term referring to how people feel about their effectiveness relative to environmental problems, and whether they are responsible for such problems.

Winett, Leckliter, Chin, and Stahl (1984), in a field experiment, sought to show that mediated information can be successful in inducing change in energy consumption behavior. Although significant change for the better (i.e., less energy consumption) was found, the media stimulus was accompanied by extensive personal contact, making the presumed power of the media unclear. Winett et al. acknowledged that these results can only be generalized to similar situations, where "intensive methods are used to insure a large audience of interested people" (p. 48).

McLeod, Glynn, and Griffin (1987) also examined the effects of energy information on energy conservation. They found that issue *salience* is associated with media use, but variables such as knowledge gain, energy attitude (pro- or anticonservation), and behavior were little influenced by specific energy media use. They could only partially support the hypothesis that public affairs programming and specific energy media content have any effect on energy conservation. They argued that "designers of programs should not assume that if they can simply affect general conservation knowledge, salience, or even attitudes, that conserving behavior will necessarily follow" (p. 33).

Griffin (1989) also found that media portrayals of environmental problems seem to have more effect on the perceived importance of an issue, without much effect on conservation behavior. Energy conservation behavior was better predicted by requests for more specific pieces of information such as pamphlets, which are seen as having the ability to answer an environmental question directly.

Griffin (1990) also examined relationships between energy information consumption and energy awareness and knowledge. He found that education level predicted knowledge about energy issues, a well-known phenomenon for all sorts of environmental issues. Griffin surmised that this should be associated with the knowledge gap, a difference in knowledge produced by mass media information campaigns that are overabsorbed by the advantaged classes. However, in his 5-year Wisconsin survey, the gap diminished, suggesting that media coverage decreased over the same period, regressing all survey respondents to the mean of energy knowledge. Griffin also found a "negative relationship of television energy information processing to energy knowledge among the better educated" (p. 565).

Finally, Brother, Fortner, and Mayer (1991) determined that media coverage could be linked to increasing knowledge about environmental issues. Their results showed that news coverage of Great Lakes issues did increase knowledge of those issues among their sample, although starting from an already rather knowledgeable base.

Many people believe that television programs such as *National Geographic* or the Cousteau specials have played an important role in raising a generation of environmentalists. Fortner and Lyon (1985) found that a Cousteau television special did have some effect in changing viewers' knowledge and opinions about environmental issues. However, these effects, emerging as they did from a single program, eroded over time, so the idea that individual programs contribute to broader ideological changes was not tested.

The agenda-setting hypothesis has also received some attention in the environmental area. Atwater, Salwen, and Anderson (1985) found that the agenda setting does apply to environmental issues. That is, media agendas seem to at least correlate with public agendas. In particular, they noted that the environmental case shows that this process extends to the "subissue" level, such that individual aspects of environmental problems become more salient as they receive coverage.

Suhonen (1993) examined the connections between coverage of the environment in Finnish newspapers and the extent of public opinion support for environmentalism. He noted that the connection between coverage of environmental issues and environmental concern is negligible. His analysis says that a "stable exogenic" model of causality makes sense in the case of environmentalism. That is, various social forces cooperate to produce a certain level of environmentalism at any given time, whereas media coverage does not produce major shifts over time, except in the case of catastrophic events.

Ader (1993, 1995) also found that the agenda-setting hypothesis can be supported for environmental issues. More interestingly, however, she compared media environmental agendas to real-world pollution states to see if increasing levels of pollution motivate increased coverage. She found the reverse: Decreases in pollution throughout the 1970s and 1980s have been accompanied by increases in media coverage. Ader did not address whether increased media coverage should in any way be held responsible for decreased pollution levels. She also found no relationship between public issue salience and real-world pollution levels.

Effects from risk portrayals in the media have also been evaluated. Sandman, Weinstein, and Klotz (1987) noted that effects of media coverage are not often based on scientific "reality." Examining natural radon risk versus industrial radon risk, they found that consumers were likely to be more outraged by industrial radon sources, even though they were far less risky than naturally occurring sources. Public response was determined to be a function of social factors such as "outrage." When it could be determined that someone's interest was being subverted by someone with a profit agenda, for instance, the media could find a news peg to hang the issue on. The authors noted that "High-outrage, low-hazard risks will provoke stronger reaction from the public than from the experts. High-hazard, low-outrage risks will provoke a stronger reaction from the experts than from the public" (p. 107).

Erfle, McMillan, and Grofman (1989) found that news media presentations of environmental problems such as the oil crises of the 1970s could influence private corporate behavior by virtue of the "regulatory threat" hypothesis. They found that increased portrayal of problems mitigated potentially harmful behavior of corporations in the public eye. Such a finding depends, however, on the perceived legitimacy of the regulatory threat, which was at an all-time low when they wrote their study and is still low despite President Bill Clinton and Vice President Albert Gore's publicized commitment to environmental cleanup.

Mikami, Takeshita, Nakada, and Kawabata (1995) assessed effects both from newspaper coverage and environment-specific television coverage in Japan around the period of the United Nations Conference on Environment and Development Rio conference in 1992. They found relatively strong correlations between the newspaper agenda for environmental issues and the public's agenda, especially when measured at a 6-to-10-week lag. They also found that those who viewed more environment-specific television material were more likely to support an environmental tax. Although they portrayed this as a test of the cultivation hypothesis (which we explore later in this book), they did not test effects from general television exposure; thus theirs is not a cultivation test.

Indeed, it is more likely that Mikami's finding simply means that environmentalists pay more attention to the environment on TV. In this area, Larson, Zimmerman, and Scherer (1984) examined media use by environmentalists as compared to nonenvironmentally active individuals. They hypothesized that those most concerned with the environment would tend to use specialized media for environmental issues more often. However, "the data . . . suggest the environmental activists do not differ from the non-active respondents in habitual mass media use, except in magazine use and in wanting to find out more about important environmental issues" (p. 19). Yet, studies of a selected sample of environmental activists show that these individuals use broadcast media far less frequently.

Ostman and Parker (1986/1987) also examined the use made by the public of information sources for environmental information. They determined that newspapers were the primary source of information for environmental news, although their sample was from Ithaca, New York, an educated community with relatively less TV coverage than many cities. Television was the second most prevalent source, followed by magazines, and then books. Peer conversation was the important source of interpersonal communication of environmental information. Books, although not the primary source, were most highly rated in terms of believability, although many respondents felt that environmental news was highly sensationalized. Also, the authors found that TV use for environmental information decreased with education level. This study provides an excellent descriptive analysis, although it is probably not highly generalizable due to the limited sample.

Although not primarily an effects study, DeHaven-Smith (1988, 1991) provided an interesting alternative view to environmentalism as public opinion. Normally, we argue that environmentalism is part of a fundamental political ideological system more or less shared by all people. DeHaven-Smith argued, on the other hand, that environmental attitudes are actually rapidly changing responses to elite political discourse, screened by personal considerations and impact on one's own personal convenience. In this view, environmentalism can only be understood *in situ*, with a knowledge of local discourse on the issue. This theoretical view tends to diminish the importance of mass media because national media coverage may well be overwhelmed by local interpersonal discussion on various issues. On the other hand, if media play an important role in determining the nature of elite discourse, which is certainly possible, then elite belief systems may well be partially determined by mass media.

This review of studies reveals a number of shortcomings in our understanding of the effects of mass communication for the environment. Obviously, most efforts have been focused on cognitions, attitudes, and behaviors. Fewer studies have dealt with environmental ideology—what we are calling the *social environment*. This is partly due to the fact that the procedures commonly used for measurement in mass communication research favor measuring effects at the individual level.

It is startling, however, that many of the studies of the effects of individual messages and campaigns show relatively little effect, whereas the more systemic-level examinations dealing with agenda-setting theories and other macrotheories of mass communication find greater relationships. This may indicate that the effects of media are more pronounced or important at the systemic level, without necessarily affecting specific issue beliefs or behavioral decisions in the short term.

A view of media as having a systemic influence on the social environment is very attractive. Theories of media effects such as cultivation (discussed later in this volume; Gerbner & Gross, 1976; Gerbner, Gross, Morgan, & Signorelli, 1982, 1994; Morgan, 1982), argue that many of the important effects of media such as television are found at a broader rather than individual level. Returning to our distinction between the social construction of the environment by individuals and the objectified social environment, it may be that research has not shown conclusive effects because it tends to look at the shallower level where such effects are less present. A variety of studies has begun to emerge that deals with this question, however, and although these studies are less empirical and more speculative, it is precisely the deeper systemic issue they address.

ENVIRONMENTAL IDEOLOGY, TECHNOLOGY, AND CULTURE

The third basic area of research deals with environmental ideologies, working at the level of analysis we identified as the *social environment*. Communication research has made recent forays into this area, especially in an attempt to widen its scope, examining cultural issues as well as media-specific problems. However, these studies also strain the boundaries of communication research in the environmental area. After all, most of the classic studies of environmentalism and the idea of nature are themselves essentially cultural criticisms. Because of this, it has been fairly difficult to distinguish what cultural media critics think about the role of media specifically in the environmental problem; they generally eschew variable-oriented studies, and there is a paucity of empirical data in these kinds of studies. Thus, although critical studies have the virtue of extending theory, assessing the role of media apart from other cultural factors within such studies is difficult. Of course, this may simply reflect real social conditions in that media have no impacts outside of the cultural context.

Downs (1972), well-known for his economic theory of democracy, articulated a mainstream view of environmental ideology in his "Up and Down with Ecology—The 'Issue-Attention' Cycle."

He viewed environmentalism as an issue that passes through the following phases: a preproblem stage leading to a period of "alarmed discovery," in which "euphoric enthusiasm" is mustered to combat the problem. Public opinion then realizes the cost of making significant progress, and a decline of intense public interest follows, leading to a postproblem phase that starts the cycle again.

How prescient was Downs' analysis? Certainly Downs wrote in a period of high public concern with the environment, and clearly environmentalism did decline drastically in the period after Downs wrote, especially in the early 1980s (although public opinion analysts have noted a broad and linear upswing in environmental opinions over the years (Dunlap, 1992; Dunlap & Mertig, 1992; Dunlap & Scarce, 1991). Then environmentalism seemed to increase in the late 1980s and early 1990s, and is in decline in the mid-1990s.

All of this depends on public opinion polls, in which people tend to "say" they are environmentally concerned (Gillroy & Shapiro, 1986). Still, for us, the historical evidence on the decline in environmentalism in the 1970s and 1990s is strong enough to confirm anecdotal impressions; it was probably caused by the general decline in attention to traditional communitarian issues during the individual feeding frenzy of that decade. The phoenix-like rise of environmentalism from these ashes of the Reagan years was in fact partly precipitated, as Downs proposed, by catastrophic environmental events, especially the major drought and hot years of the late 1980s. The period from 1988 to 1992 is identifiable as the height of this "second wave" of concern. Now however, we see evidence of a second decline coming from number of areas.

R. Morgan (1992) highlighted the new decline:

> The Earth had its Day last week, but nobody noticed. Or so it seems when compared to the hoopla of Earth Day 1990. Back then, when consciousness was so elevated *Time* bestowed its most-watched cover to the "Planet of the Year," everybody was in the act. The Day itself was celebrated by millions of consumers, dozens of corporate sponsors and more PSA's than an environmentally correct citizen should see.

> Green marketers could do no wrong, causing violators as diverse as McDonald's and P&G not only to see green but to act green. "The environment is not a fad," their flacks would say. "We know this issue isn't going away."

> In a mere two weeks, the print media churned out 30% of all environmental stories between Earth Days 1990 and 1991, according to Fairness and Accuracy In Reporting. The same two weeks also saw network news devote more than 40% of the air

time the environment would receive all year. No doubt much of this "reporting glut," as FAIR calls it in its current Extra! publication, stems from the special 20th-anniversary status of Earth Day 1990. A year later, interest had fallen so that Extra! headlined its analysis of environmental reporting "The Big Fizzle." The decline continued through last week, so that Earth Day 1992 might be remembered-if remembered at all—as the Little Poof. (p. 52)

By 1994, certainly, the trumpet calls had echoed into the wilderness, and fewer were hearing them. The Boston *Globe* announced "Fanfare Fades, but Awareness, Actions Increase" (1994). Environmental "actions" were things like recycling, which certainly did increase, although probably as much as a function of economic necessity than anything else. As far as media hype, however, the green had faded to brown. It seemed as if the environment could not escape the vicissitudes of the public opinion roller coaster, presumably exacerbated by media patterns of coverage.

Broader relationships between media and ideology must be brought to bear to try to understand such cyclical patterns. Wiebe (1973), borrowing on the "narcotization" notion prevalent in some media effects research, argued that mass media would produce a sense of "well-informed futility" in its viewership about environmental issues. He said that the mediation process itself is of prime importance because this tends to draw us away from the real environment ("unless it is perceived as being in one's own scene, it is not experienced as fully real" [p. 428]). Wiebe also was one of the first to note the possibility that "attention" to environmental issues can still distract from larger overall problems: "While children clean up a square mile, a corporation or municipality pollutes a square mile" (p.429).

Pirages and Ehrlich (1974) suggested that the DSP embedded in the media stresses traditional beliefs and values emphasizing progress, technology, production, and materialism. Their analysis also suggests that media play their role at a deeper, paradigmatic level. If correct, this suggests that the best question to ask is not how media change environmental opinions and attitudes, but how media maintain and strengthen the existing paradigm, the existing social environment.

Dunlap and Van Liere (1984) examined this issue quantitatively: They found a negative correlation between measures of attachment to the DSP and degree of environmental concern. Thus, the current dominant way of thinking still is anti-environmental.

Despite this, public opinion surveys show a consistently high level of support for environmental protection (Gillroy &

Shapiro, 1986). For instance, more than 50% of respondents to the General Social Survey (GSS) have consistently said that too little is spent on the natural environment. This may simply mean that people will support anything on a public opinion survey, or it may mean that rudimentary environmental concern is developing throughout the populace. Perhaps it is some of both.

These observations about "background" cultural attention to environmental issues help us to think about better ways to examine mediated effects on the social environment. Lowe and Morrison (1984), studying the British coverage of environmentalism, noted that environmentalism as an ideology has been able to attract media attention because it can be treated as a depoliticized issue. Saving baby seals or building national parks can be graphically interesting stories with heavy emotional content. Although these stories sometimes threaten individual actors within the corporate capitalist ideology, they do not in fact radically threaten the ideology itself. Thus, media support for environmentalism is primarily due to the characteristics of these stories one can tell about the environment. As they noted:

> Should the environmental lobby ever become more radical in praxis or militant in tactics such that it became seen as posing a serious threat to the existing order, then it is probable that it would have to contend with a more skeptical and less sympathetic environmental order. (p. 88)

The example of a group such as Earth First! would seem to confirm this analysis. Lowe and Morrison's analysis shows how media "attention" to environmental issues need not be confused with paradigmatic change.

Hepburn and Hepburn (1985) examined the political dimension of the environmental controversy when they studied the case of Canadian films on acid rain that were denied entry into the United States. Because acid rain was a sensitive issue in U.S.-Canadian politics in the 1980s, it was revealing when the U.S. Justice Department labeled the film, "Requiem or Recovery" (a Canadian film critical of acid rain), *propaganda*. The authors argued that the decision of the Reagan administration was manifestly political, although recent evidence on the acid rain controversy has shown that there is indeed more than one side to this story (McComas, 1994). In any case, environmentalism is an ideal issue for the cultural theorists who argue that media presentations are essentially founded on political readings pregiven by power elites.

Despite elite control of media, there are outlets for environmental opposition. Downing (1988) articulated a concept of the *alternative public sphere* relative to the environment. This idea proposes that oppositional forces within society do have the ability to articulate for themselves a space within which their own discourse can be privileged and their own knowledge pursued. This is fairly important for environmentalism, which has primarily been a movement of opposition. This especially relates to the importance of media for environmentalism because the conception explicitly shows that there are other ways for environmentalists to win recruits than through the commercial mass media.

Cracknell (1993) argued that a limitation exists in a media-based approach to environmental problems. Because the use of the media by issue-interest groups can encounter various hurdles, and because some very successful issue groups keep a low profile, a media-based approach tends to overstate the importance of public communication in solving environmental problems. Therefore, media theorists should keep in mind that media constitute only one of the public arenas for discourse on environmental problems.

This suggests that the media participate in cultural processes more complex than those analyzed by the media effects theorists. Burgess (1989) articulated this when she said that "My central proposition is that the media industry is participating in a complex, cultural process through which environmental meanings are produced and consumed" (p. 139). Few would deny the truth of this kind of assertion, although it is not immediately evident what this proposition gains us. Just exactly how the complex cultural processes work in producing environmental meaning is knowledge we still do not have.

It is important to remember that the new critical research is a response to old effects research, which was often absurdly behavioristic and reductionistic. It is fairly clear that some sort of rapprochement is needed between critical and empirical approaches, to avoid the determinism of one and the tendencies toward trivial tautology of the other. We should note here that our criticisms of the critical research tradition are meant to be constructive, because they offer something to the empirically flavored media research sorely needed: a connection to social reality.

As another example of the critical approach, Burgess et al. (Burgess & Harrison, 1993; Burgess, Harrison, & Maiteny, 1991) made a study of coverage of a nature conservation problem in the United Kingdom. This study is a classic example of a culturally critical "reading" of a "text," in this case about preserving some marshland from commercial development. They found that media coverage was interpreted in different ways by different audiences. One intent of this kind of study is to decrease the insistence that mass media coverage will have unitary effects. In this particular case, one important reading was that both corporate representatives and environmentalists could be seen by audiences as "elitist outsiders."

The media effects theory known as *technological determinism* proposes that the real impact of media is a "formal" effect that becomes known when new technologies appear. The best known proponent of this theory was Marshall McLuhan. In the environmental area, a technological determinist might argue that media technologies tend to "remove" people from their natural environment and therefore deprive them of knowledge they might otherwise have. This idea has been incorporated in Green philosophies, also reflecting the Luddism common in certain strains of environmentalism. Bachmair (1991) gave a rather interesting version of this thesis, connecting the development of television to the social function served by automobiles. He argued that television serves the need for individualized mobility, originally "created" by the automobile. The connection to consumer capitalism is clear, particularly the highly individual version promoted and instantiated in the United States. Bachmair said that "Television succeeded because it broadened and extended lifestyles associated with the motorcar: primarily those associated with mobility as a shaping principle of communication" (p. 522). If this is true, an environmental effect of television should be to encourage greater personal movement in all phases of life, with concomitant impacts in areas greater mobility would require, such as in air pollution.

As noted earlier, Hansen (1991, 1993a, 1993b) gave the most complete and compelling view of what environmental mass communication research could look like in the future. He is certainly disenchanted with the "linear" effects research characterizing much of the research on environmental media effects. However, he was careful to avoid the trap of trivial tautology by directing research questions to places where real answers can be expected. As an example, media researchers can examine cultural "resonances" in the production of environmental stories. Instead of simply assuming that information flows from producers to consumers, researchers could examine the production of particular meanings as a social process. The key here is that critical researchers must still preserve a view of the media as somewhat powerful, that is, as having some ability to characterize stories in particular ways. The twist is that audiences themselves may not accept the particular coding proffered by the media, choosing a different reading. But the idea to choose a different reading may itself be contexted by media choices in storytelling. Thus, media "power" may reside at many different junctures and levels.

This reasoning suggests that identifying "causes" in media effects research on the environment may well be impossible because any event of interest may be seen as being both cause and effect. The methodological problem is that isolating a single series of events that can be bracketed as possible causes and possible effects is difficult. One solution, used in this book, is to examine cross-sectional populations with the idea of discovering possible feedback loops of environmental information. Hansen is absolutely correct that the older studies of environmental effects need revision; this book may offer some revisions that can be seen as a midpoint between traditional effects studies and critical research.

THE MEDIA EFFECTS PERSPECTIVE

That the "old" media perspective is somewhat outdated is evident. We probably can learn or need to learn little more about the impacts of specific messages and their role in producing specific "conservation" behaviors, such as saving energy or recycling. Common sense tells us that media promotion is certainly a valuable tool in trying to develop an ecological perspective among the population at large. On the other hand, there is certainly no science of persuasion allowing us to "produce" environmentalism among audiences as a matter of policy; there are simply too many variables to consider and too many social and political factors to consider as well.

The response of the constructionists is often to ignore effects completely, at least at the individual level. They would pay attention to how media "construct" social realities relevant to environmentalism, with a more abstracted concern for the macrolevel cultural readings of environmental issues, which are possible given the plethora of media messages devoted to nature and the natural. The most common problem here is that the research tends to be highly self-contained and not immediately generative of specific conclusions. There is too much of a temptation to be fascinated by the new social jargon to see that, often, nothing more is said than "media are important to constructing attitudes about the environment." But realistically, that statement needs to be a starting place.

As a compromise, a media effects perspective that does not ignore potential "linear" effects and can also account for relativistic aspects of social constructionism is needed. Such an approach would have three characteristics. First, it would eschew causality. Inasmuch as the environment itself is a system without a specific starting point, so is a system of environmental communication a nested series of relationships without start or end. To ask which messages "produce" which effects is a question that may not make sense. Examining the relations between messages and various states of the system would be better. Rather than "explaining" the relations causally, we could "characterize" them systemically. Media effects research without "effects" may seem somewhat illogical, although we could adopt the notion that "uses" of media are like effects (Lull, 1986).

Second, the research must be able to pay attention to the important "units" of communication. If any conclusion is inherent in most of the environmental communication studies, it is that "stories" are the relevant unit of analysis. Specific "messages" such as promotional announcements, campaigns, and advertisements tend to be lost within the more meaningful framework of narrative structures that really help people understand their environment. Thus, to simply analyze messages is to miss the forest for the old-growth trees. To avoid this problem, we must pay attention to the substance of the communicative flow. Although we may wish to speak in glittering generalities about deep-seated ideologies and politically privileged readings, we must have an empirical basis to our arguments. Thus, to simply theorize is not enough, there must be confirmation of our views in real events that everyone can agree count as data in such an analysis. In the next chapter, we argue that "stories" are the relevant unit of analysis allowing us a middle perspective; neither overtheorized nor too microanalytic, the story is a relevant unit of meaning for all members of our society.

Finally, media effects research needs to find more ways to account effectively for "readings." Readings are the presumably different interpretations given to texts by audiences. There is currently a significant body of literature on readings, which carries the problem of most qualitative research: generalizability. Media effects research, which has a mandate to seek generalizability, must account for differential readings without destroying the overall edifice of the research. Although it is tempting to argue there are as many individual readings as individuals, there clearly are broader trends which emerge only after macrosocial study. Although the theorists of the differential reading have generally studiously avoided macrosocial research, we argue that media effects research still needs to retain this focus. Thus, the survey research approach can account for developments in the theory of reading texts by actually accounting for the nature of different readings in terms of which are widely accepted or not. The notion of "preferred reading," then, explicitly legitimizes a macrosocial approach to media effects data.

In the next chapters, we endeavor to bridge an empirical and a critical perspective. Informed by this review of the literature, the rest of this book attempts two things: First, to characterize the relationship between media stories and the environment, and second, to theorize the nature of these relationships. How directly do stories relate to conceptions? How directly do institutions condition stories? How open are environmental stories to revision? What is the relationship among stories, conceptions, and real-world systemic states? Can productive change be induced? These questions include many of the answers given in the preceding literature review, although newer questions are included as well.

To answer these questions, chapter 3 looks at stories and the environment from a narrative perspective. Some historical comments about "traditional" narrative are offered, and some of the literature on narrative rationality is examined, as well.

The point is to determine how stories were and are used in everyday life to make everyday decisions. Obviously, these decisions affected the environment as well, in that the stories are both symptomatic of and determinative of the social environment. In times when "media" did not exist, it may not have made sense to ask what "caused" attitudes and beliefs, but stories undoubtedly played a major role. Our analysis will show how the stories we tell today, although embedded in media, serve virtually the same function.

three

NARRATIVES, COMMUNICATION AND THE ENVIRONMENT

In this chapter we look at differences and similarities in storytelling systems, and how these differences and similarities may affect environmental conceptions. In chapter 4, we begin a quantitative critical analysis of the impacts of modern story systems on environmental consciousness. In this chapter, we attempt to undergird that analysis with a discussion of theoretical issues related to narratives and narrative cultures. Specifically, we consider how story systems differ across certain kinds of cultures, and we connect these differences to issues that tend to arise when we consider television as an environmental storyteller.

   If we adopt a perspective on mass media as a mechanism for modern "myth delivery," it is not a leap to see television and other mass media as an extension of a very ancient social institution: the local storyteller. And if television merely extends a culturally universal and socially constructive role, it is also reasonable that a commentary on how "ancient" or "primitive" stories affected environmental conceptions might be relevant for an understanding of the relationship between television's narrative myths and today's environmental conceptions.

In this chapter we look at pre-media story systems to better understand how to think about today's important media such as television, newspapers, news magazines, and other forms. Although we do not provide a complete theoretical or anthropological account of how stories function culturally (which would be beyond the scope of this volume), we do look at a few interesting issues to provide a measure of perspective on the role played by today's media systems.

THEORIES OF NARRATIVE AND THEIR MEANING FOR THE ENVIRONMENT

Current psychological research shows that the ideological aspects of environmental thought are extremely important in the temporally "later" determination of relatively more ephemeral "attitudes" or "opinions" (e.g., Gray, 1985). Ideologies, belief systems, and the "dominant social paradigm" are therefore extensively implicated in people's responses to current environmental issues and problems. Yet these ideologies, like attitudes and opinions, also "come from" somewhere, and some type of information "work" must occur to create and maintain them. What is the source and place of this work? We think that, even today, narratives are where this work occurs.

We have suggested that there are really two aspects to our environmental beliefs. First, the social construction of the environment contains opinions about "things" or issues. Second, the social environment contains deeper cultural codings and linkages that influence our perceptions of the environment. At the level of social construction, "informational" messages can give us what we need to formulate opinions about environmental issues. But such messages do not really deal with the individual as "subject." Thomashow (1995) indicated that developing an environmental or ecological "identity" is a key issue for those who see themselves as "environmentalists." In Thomashow's perspective, an environmental identity is the simple but important idea that "people construe themselves in relationship to the Earth as manifested in personality, values, actions, and sense of self. Nature becomes an object of identification" (p. 3). But we would note that all individuals, either very consciously or through processes of social constructions, accept some knowledge or wisdom about their position in the environment, whether or not they see themselves as environmentalists.

To construct our own position within an environment, we need to have access to stories that give coherent accounts of what people with recognized characteristics do in a variety of situations. In an important sense, our understanding of our own position within a moral and environmental order often comes from a narrative understanding in which characters play particular dramatic roles. If stories have any impact on our environmental conceptions, it is as much through locating us as subjects in an environment as through delivering environmental information and lessons. We argue that stories influence our perceptions especially at the deeper level of the social environment. One of the mechanisms of this influence is through a process of *identity construction* for individuals.

But there is more to identity than awareness of self. Identities cannot be constituted or "built" by individuals alone. To be socially relevant, identities must be agreed upon constructs that allow individuals to pursue goals in the real world. For example, *environmentalist* is not an identity developed through the simple reflective process of one individual; it comes from a dialectical social process that constructs the meaning of that identity. In such a social process, behaviors appropriate for that identity are "assigned." The person searching for a more meaningful identity may then grasp environmentalism as providing more meaning, but we should not lose sight of the term's socially constructed status. This means that environmental identities, like any other identity, can come from narratives. In fact, narratives may be among the most powerful sources for the construction of environmental identity.

We assume that narratives guide identity construction and selection. Bormann (1985), like some others, accounts for the meaning inherent in social groupings and identities through an analysis of shared narratives. In Bormann's theory of "symbolic convergence" (building on theories such as the symbolic interactionism of George Herbert Mead and Charles Horton Cooley), the appearance of group consciousness is an outcome of shared social experiences of narration. Shared fantasies provide group members with comprehensible forms for explaining their past and thinking about their future—a basis for communication and for group consciousness.

Narratives cannot exist without "characters," which give narrative form to identity. Indeed, the "normal" narrative type has "good" and "bad" characters involved in a series of events with a linear, unfolding, temporal dimension (Aristotle's "beginning, middle, and end"). Characters' identities are described by their actions within the context of the plot. Their goodness or badness is made manifest to "involve" the audience, which can be gripped, fearful, in suspense, laughing, or angry, or more. These narratively defined identities can be seen as a stock supply of characters that individuals potentially choose from in interpreting their own life. In this way, the narrative, which can teach only a finite number of lessons, can constitute characters who will act in known ways in an almost infinite number of situations.

Thus, identities, which constitute individuals, are not unlike beliefs and attitudes held by individuals in that they are both socially constituted. Yet they are different as well. An "ideology" is a system of beliefs; an identity is a perception about who one is and where one fits in the world. Ideologies and identities obviously interact in the description of various behaviors and beliefs.

In the environmental sphere, there are many different ideological beliefs, as well as many different possible identities. For instance, environmentalists of fairly similar ideological persuasion, such as members of Earth First! and the Green Party, may crucially differ in their identity perception, because Green Party members identify themselves as "within the system," whereas members of Earth First! see themselves as "without." Similarly, ideological differences can be well accommodated within the environmental movement because both conservatives and liberals can coexist as environmentalists, partly because of the similar political identities they hold.

Still, the environmentalist identity seems to appeal to a growing number of individuals. Much of the success of the environmental identity is due to the excellent storytellers who have told their story in the mass media. John Muir, the founding guru of the Sierra Club and wilderness protection pioneer, was a best-selling storyteller. Rachel Carson's *Silent Spring*, although relying on science, used metaphor so effectively that her ideas about the dangers of pesticides could not be ignored and helped to launch a movement. Aldo Leopold, founder of the "land ethic" and prototypical radical environmentalist, told his environmental story through the eyes of a dying wolf. Each storyteller, through powerful narration and imagery, established for themselves a morally worthy social position that others wanted to emulate. These constructed environmental identities, established and given worth in the communication crucible of the mass media, are what lend such power to environmentalism today.

THE IMPORTANCE OF NARRATIVE

Although few dispute the power of narrative, the literature on mass communication of the environment disparages the narrational quality of much of that communication. The literature often suggests that environmental "facts," discovered by science, are twisted into interesting stories by the narration industries (i.e., the mass media). The environmental mass communication studies seen in chapter 2 suggest that the end result is that people don't "learn" what they are supposed to about the environment.

Such studies tend to assume that humans characteristically use a scientific or technical rationality when they make judgments about the environment, or at least that they should use such a rationality. Fisher (1984), however, developed one of the more cogent arguments showing that this is not the case. Naming humans *homo narrans* (storytelling Man), Fisher viewed narration as the fundamental constituent of human rationality. He located narration in "a theory of symbolic actions—words and/or deeds— that have sequences and meaning for those who live, create, or interpret them" (p. 2). As such, narrative is relevant to both reality and fiction. Fisher's narrative paradigm presupposes:

> (1) humans are essentially storytellers; (2) the paradigmatic mode of human decision-making and communication is "good reasons" which vary in form among communication situations, genres, and media; (3) the production and practice of good reasons is ruled by matters of history, biography, culture, and character. . . ; (4) rationality is determined by the nature of persons as narrative beings—their inherent awareness of "narrative probability," what constitutes a coherent story, and their constant habit of testing "narrative fidelity," whether the stories they experience ring true with the stories they know to be true in their lives. . . . (5) the world is a set of stories which must be chosen among to live the good life in a process of continual recreation; . . . the materials of the narrative paradigm are symbols, signs of consubstantiation, and good reasons, the communicative expressions of social reality. (pp. 7-8)

When narrative is taken as the "master metaphor" (p. 6), it subsumes other metaphors which "recount" (e.g., history, biography, or bibliography) or "account" for (e.g., legal explanations) human choice and action. "[E]ach mode of recounting and accounting for is but a way of relating a 'truth' about the human condition" (p. 6). Fisher's idea is that "symbols are created and communicated ultimately as stories meant to give order to human experience and to induce others to dwell in them to establish ways of living in common, in communities in which there is sanction for the story that constitutes one's life" (p. 6).

Fisher (1984) compared and contrasted this view with the traditional "rational" perspective on symbolic interaction. The rational world paradigm presumes that:

(1) humans are essentially rational beings, (2) the paradigmatic
mode of human decision-making and communication is argument, . . . (3) the conduct of argument is ruled by the dictates of
situations, . . . (4) rationality is determined by subject matter
knowledge, argumentative ability and skill in employing the
rules of advocacy in given fields, and (5) that the world is a set
of logical puzzles which can be resolved through appropriate
analysis and application of reason. (p. 4; also see Fisher, 1985,
1987, 1988)

Fisher's view is one in which people behave in narratively
"rational" ways that make sense to them based on the stories they
hear and tell. These are the "good reasons." Although the good reasons may not make sense from the perspective of scientists and
technical experts, they almost universally make sense to those who
use them. These good reasons are accepted because they "hang
together" with the stories that people use and understand. Thus,
narrative "integrity," the extent to which a story makes sense to the
listener, is an important variable that can determine why people do
or do not accept statements and arguments as true or false.

For instance, to portray the Exxon *Valdez* situation as a
collection of facts regarding an oil spill and its effects would not
interest many people. Consider, for instance, other oil spills that
have not excited as much interest or concern. But to thread together the Exxon *Valdez* "story," complete with "villains" such as
Captain Joseph Hazelwood and the anonymous Exxon Corporation,
"innocent victims" such as the Alaska fishermen and natives, and a
plot line with a beginning, middle, and end, draws in many more
listeners and readers who can find and understand the narrative
rationality; the *Valdez* story exemplifies a time-tested narrative
principle. Suspense, guilt, punishment, remorse: All these factors
will come to bear on a person's eventual understanding of what
"happened" in Prince William Sound.

We argue that narrative rationality is very important for
environmental understandings, as environmental communication
research is beginning to show. But surprisingly, relatively little of
this research has explored the principles of narrative theory with
respect to our environmental understandings. We attempt to
explore these concepts in the next paragraphs, bearing in mind the
following hypothesis: People's understandings of their environment
and their role in it emerge from personal experience with narratives
and their enmeshment in such narratives.

"PLACE"

Having already established that *identity* is an important environmental construct, and that rationality is often a narrative issue, we next examine the issue of *place*, obviously an important environmental matter. A person's perception of place is, in some sense, coextensive with his or her concept of environment. Yet where we are is also a socially constructed concept, different from our simple physical location. Our narrative impacts on place are also important to consider, particularly because technology allows us to amplify those impacts.

Meyerowitz's (1985) argument is perhaps the best known position that media and forms of communication contribute to our sense of place. Specifically, Meyrowitz argued that media forms tend to damage our sense of place. McKibben (1992) also argued that massive attention to television and other mediated discourse tends to remove us from a natural setting, putting us in a different place. These arguments display a kind of technological determinism in which the power of certain forms of communication accrues from their ability to dominate consciousness and alter the human *sensorium* (which was McLuhan's, 1964, term).

But a narrative perspective would seem to imply that narrative content and structure, rather than simply the mediated "form" of communication, also play a role in constructing a sense of place. Burke's (1945) *A Grammar of Motives* offers one of the better known examples of a narrative conception of place. Burke argued that human actions and accounts of actions are always guided by an understanding of five terms: *scene, act, agent, agency,* and *purpose.* Burke said we use a *dramatistic* logic when organizing our understanding of the world. The five terms are categories of meaning that structure human intercourse. In Burke's system, a "scene" is the background for any event in which humans attempt to do things. Burke argued that the scene "contains" the possibility of the event; the act is implicit within the scene. He said, "We may examine the term *Scene* as a blanket term for the concept of background or setting in general, a name for any situation in which agents are placed" (p. xvi). Burke imagined that scenes condition acts by implying and revealing the appropriateness of an act within a given scene. This "scene-act ratio" idea shows how background conceptions can influence story content and plot.

Extrapolating from this, we argue that a conception of the environment as a bountiful resource in the dominant narrative paradigm is a necessary scenic preconception to actions that are understood as exploiting resources for human benefit. By this logic, stories that give those lessons "require" environmental conceptions that permit the story to have meaning. Yet with the scene taking a background position, the logic of the entire act is less likely to be questioned, because it is the "act" itself that is usually justified in our thinking, not the scene. Scenes exist; they are a given; they do not need to be justified.

This conception relates to a view espoused by Barthes (1957), which is that discourse tends to "naturalize History." That is, human "act" and "agency" tend to produce and then reinforce conceptions of what is "natural," removing any tinge of human agency from it in the process. This tendency to build "common-sense" understandings of the world through discourse is what gives the scene its inevitabilistic tinge.

Neither Burke nor Barthes was thinking specifically of "the environment" in their discussions of nature and scene. But the narrative possibilities for an interpretive understanding of nature are endless. The implication is that we build conceptions of nature that suit our dramatic/narrative purposes. From this perspective, environmentalism is a philosophy or set of stories that requires a conception of the environment as a being with rights, purposes, and so on. That is, the conception of the environment (as scene) emerges from the narrative purpose, not the other way around.

Now it would be naive and simplistic to imagine that our conception of the environment as a scene is formed only by narrative strategies. As we already argued, the natural environment is a system that eventually shapes and constructs the social environments built on top of it. But Burke's and Barthes' ideas give us access to an important tool for analyzing the contribution of story systems to environmental conceptions: Human actions are relevant to conceptions of nature, because conceptions of nature are chosen partly to legitimize human actions. Thus, to the extent that we understand the point and purpose of a story, we must understand how that story emerged from its scenic requirements.

For the analysis of mass media effects, this means that background images and themes are just as important as foreground portrayals. It means that we must look for conceptions of nature throughout the media system to see whether there are consistencies in scenic depiction and whether these consistencies can be legitimately connected to the purpose of the stories being told. An important question for this book is whether nature, the scene par excellence, is pushed into the background by other scenes that emphasize human-centeredness.

We conceive of stories as a means of enforcing social environmental conceptions. The same is true for most cultural conceptions. However, as seen in chapter 4, modern stories do not emphasize natural themes, nor does the manner of our telling stories have the function of connecting us to the environment as a relevant scene for our actions. The way we tell stories tends to emphasize the social and physical connections not of the natural world, but of a technocratic, bureaucratic, and mediacentric society. Human scenes replace natural scenes more and more frequently.

Historically, traditional stories acted as cultural regulators, maintaining and reconstructing the cultural order of the timeless age. The scene for such stories was normally a holistic mixture of society, culture, identity, and the natural world. As Western rationality developed, more complex and differentiated cultural structures required systems of logic (i.e., scenes) to explain them. The rapidly proliferating levels of society required individuals (agents) to be increasingly separated from their natural environment, and the individual character in a story or narrative began to assume many more of the dramatic needs of the piece. That in itself began to cultivate the Western sense of the importance of the individual as a decision-making and autonomous agent in a space of other such agents, as opposed to a member of a culture intricately linked to all other members of the culture. Increasingly, other humans and human-made constructs could come to serve as their own scene. Thus, social differentiation is as responsible for the loss of "sense of place" as the technological facts of various new media developments. As individuals began to distinguish themselves from each other, they also began to distinguish themselves from their natural context (Evernden, 1992, made the same argument when he connected the development of the very concept of nature to the development of rational thought systems in the Classical world).

The role of the great storytelling media systems in constructing and enforcing these new social conceptions is one place to search for the sources of new conceptions of nature. With the rise of mass media, storytelling systems emerged whose purpose was commercial gain. The discovery of the enormous power that accrues from connecting narrative skill to mercenary goals has contexted the entire development of the mass media. With commercial gain understood as the ultimate purpose of most stories (recalling that Burke established "purpose" as a vital component of his "pentad"), we can hypothesize that media systems had to develop scenic conceptions that would fund the eventual motive of commercial gain. That is, actors would have to be placed in scenes that would legitimize consumption, work, profit, and adherence to a broad set of middle-class values in which wealth and money would be the final arbiters of value. With individual work and achievement a dominant way to evaluate worth, the inherent environmental value of resources would be diminished. In a sense, to highlight individual achievement, one must downplay the value of natural resources.

It is very much the person, the "self," the "hero" and his or her (usually his) individual motives and actions that begin to take the foreground in the modern media story. The individual conception of personhood requires a background of things that are "not the person." These forces act on the person as scene, and they may include natural forces or forces set in motion by other individuals. The great story of Western culture, or at least a great story, is of the heroic individual who meets threats from a variety of sources, defining the source of cultural excellence as emerging from the individual. The hero faces threats representing tasks that must be faced by the culture as well. The excellence of the hero increases in proportion to the severity of the challenge. Stronger individuals come from more "dangerous" environments. Whether challenged in war, or in journey, or in spirit, our view of the protagonist depends quite strongly on how we see his or her environment challenging that person. The increasing importance of the individual as the focus of the story necessarily means that collective identities are glossed, whereas the environment is either demonized (as challenge to the hero) or ignored.

Modern media stories hitch this individual meeting of cultural and environmental challenges to a bourgeois purpose. The backgrounding of the environment as challenge to the individual is meant to underline that individuals always face challenges and must work hard in a heartless world to overcome them. At the same time, such messages support power and political structures that guarantee order for those without the nerve to stand alone. The dialectic of danger and power enhances belief in a system whose ultimate arbiter is the monetary elite. In chapter 4 we analyze how television stories conform to this structure.

Of course, the increasing individualization in Western storytelling does not mean that the nature story disappears. But it clearly metamorphosed to accommodate the needs of modernizing society. The theme of the individual against nature appeared with increasing frequency, when nature appeared at all. The Biblical story of Genesis explicitly placed Man and Nature in opposing positions, giving us a narrative reason why life in the wilderness is difficult; the world is constructed as a wilderness in which individuals must prove themselves by adherence to abstract principles of religious loyalty. Nature, once seen by some as provider, mother, and fully fledged social participant, was now seen as test, context, and enemy.

But there is apparently a residual need for the nature experience, as long as it can be packaged in a form which neither threatens civilized safety nor requires real knowledge of nor attachment to natural issues. Witness the development of the environment as "theme" in theme parks, movies, and vacation destinations around the country and indeed the world. In Disney World alone, for instance, one can experience virtually every type of natural environment, although each has been completely "imagineered" so that any aspect of verisimilitude has been removed. In any case, we are not to forget that "it's a small world after all." Even visits to "authentic" natural areas are packaged so that the experience is meaningful within the industrial late capitalist mindset. Although the urban or suburban resident could manage the temporary withdrawal from the comforts of a "normal" lifestyle, a true natural experience might produce a questioning of the commitment to the objective horrors of living within the boundaries of the dominant social paradigm. The "packaged" environmental experience provides respite without paradigmatic questioning.

Beyond "respite," the packaged environment provides a rich source of meanings and ways to connect the environment to consumer culture. Price (1995), in "Looking for Nature at the Mall," noted the increasing tendency to package "nature" as meaning for upscale consumers looking for a way to disassociate themselves from mainstream consumer culture (i.e., those seeking a way to consume without assuming the negative consequences of that consumption):

> for many of us "nature" counters consumption—"simple," "primitive," and "natural," it's a palliative for modern materialism—and the whole store flashes NATURE like a neon warning sign. If I define myself with the things I buy, I define myself also by what I think "nature" means. At the Nature Company, I am an anti-consumer consumer. (p. 198)

It is obviously too trite to present a single unified view of Western narrative understandings of the environment; the modern nature story will be found in many different forms with different morals. Indeed, it is characteristically postmodern that stories tend to break apart, with a loss of unity of perspective. In the end, not every modern telling of an environmental story can necessarily be characterized as inauthentic or destructive of a better understanding of the environment.

Partly to deal with this issue, we feel that a more systematic and quantifiable procedure is necessary for dealing with multiplicity in environmental narrative. Although particular environmental stories may vary greatly from one to another, we argue that a greater unity of perspective can be found at the level of the story system. To understand this theorized unity, the next chapter discusses cultural indicators perspectives that allow for examination of message systems. Prior to that discussion, however, we examine some narrative examples that help clarify our theoretical arguments, and deal with some issues related to the role of communication structure in narrative understanding.

COMPARATIVE STORY EFFECTS: MYTHS PRIMITIVE AND MODERN

Relationships between people and their environment are the topic for many of the earliest stories we know. The tendency to fictionalize the natural world is certainly one of humankind's most universal characteristics. Many, if not all, origin myths, for instance, are accounts or descriptions of the "received" natural world as understood by various cultures. Most such myths also include a rationalization or explanation of the role of people within the environment. The same can be said of the Judeo-Christian origin myth, found in the early chapters of Genesis in the Bible.

As we have argued, we can see our modern mass media systems as functional equivalents for these myth systems of early ages. As mass media researchers have noted (Gerbner & Gross, 1976), the television system of today has essentially replaced the earlier important myth deliverers, including the church, family, and community. The universal human desire to tell and hear stories is most served today by television (and secondarily by other mass media institutions).

Although television amplifies the frequency of storytelling and connects it to a commercial purpose, the simple act of television storytelling is not much different than the storytelling act in most "primitive" cultures. Storytelling may be one of the few universal human communication practices. People share the same stories as a function of being members of the same culture. The stories are repeated, retold, embellished, and internalized, eventually with an important effect on mental structures (what we think of as "meaning"). Thus, the cultural impact of themes in situation comedies (to take a seemingly trivial example) may be very similar to the impact of well-known mythic themes in traditional cultures. All in all, there is significant justification for examining both early myths and modern media stories as species of the same genus.

But an analysis comparing modern media effects to general "story" effects is quite difficult to achieve. Today we tend to think of the "media" (i.e., as technologies) as having effects, yet it may simply be the stories themselves that are important. Although there are many recorded examples of early myths, it is much more difficult to connect them to behavior and audience "reception," especially in the way we attempt to connect media "effects" to attitude and behavior. Of course, a large anthropological literature relates cultural narratives to cultural understandings. Much, if not most of this work, treats stories as "evidence" of cultural lifeways, mores, beliefs, and so on. However, to connect stories to their "reception" in the way that is made possible by modern social science research techniques is much more difficult for ancient stories. That is, it is somewhat more difficult to connect stories to "effects" that they would have had. Therefore, work in this field must be primarily speculative.

Today's scholarly literature is replete with historical accounts of how cultures thought, particularly in terms of the extant works produced by scholars or other writers in those early traditions. Our understanding of Greek culture, for instance, seems largely to be an understanding of elite philosophy, drama, poetry, and art (although not exclusively, as historical anthropologists continue to make progress in this area). This may tell us something about how cultural elites might have thought (and how our own culture has been influenced by them), but how much could we learn about everyday conception and treatment of the environment from those sources? An analogical problem would be trying to discover modern people's environmental conceptions only from an understanding of the works of today's elite academic philosophers. One gets the feeling that we would miss substantial information about everyday life. The problem is exacerbated in the case of very ancient cultures with no substantial written records where the disciplines of history and anthropology face even greater challenges in reconstructing the reality of a given everyday culture. Oral tradition becomes the sole means of access to these realities.

Obviously, even in our own present-day situation, with access to extensive social data and scientific research techniques, it is difficult to pin down exactly the sources and nature of environmental and social realities. At some level, therefore, the story offers itself as a unit of analysis that is much more democratic in its scope because most people in a given culture know some of the same stories and interpret them in some similar ways. Furthermore, stories can survive relatively intact, even if people's understandings of them change. An anthropologist in the year 3000, familiarized with our dominant system of storytelling (the mass media), would be able to tell much more about our conceptions of everyday reality than a scholar familiar only with the philosophy of Descartes, Marx, Freud, or Hitler. In order to understand how cultures characterize their environment, it would seem that a narrative understanding is required. Thus, although it may well be impossible completely and empirically to verify our understandings of how audiences received stories, a descriptive effort can still be worthy within the scope of this book.

Indeed, to engage in such an effort is a crucial issue for several reasons. It is common now to believe that "ancient" or "primitive" cultures lived in closer harmony with their environment. Many environmentalists would argue that primitive hunter-gatherers or pre/early agricultural societies offer us a "true" or "natural" environmentalism in their own ancient example (e.g., Oelschlager, 1991, who argued "Harmony with rather than exploitation of the natural world was a guiding principle for the Paleolithic mind and remains a cardinal commitment among modern aborigines" [p. 17]). At a spiritual, material, and technical level, the lifestyle strategies of the "primitive" have demonstrated a particularly persuasive cachet in today's environmental arguments. Some environmentalists argue, at least implicitly, that modern culture should abandon that which specifically makes it modern, so that we can "get back" to a situation with lower technology and less exploitation of nonrenewable resources.

Not surprisingly, in the context of today's environmental polemic, a particularly salient aspect of these arguments is the use of ancient stories and story types to show that primitive people understood better how to coexist harmoniously with the natural world, without trying to dominate it. Indeed, sectors of the environmental movement have adopted, adapted, and translated many of the philosophical and religious positions putatively common to more primitive cultures. For instance, Berry (1988) asserted the philosophical primacy of Native Americans not only because of their "temporal priority but by their mystical understanding and communion with the continent" (p. 181).

In our own society, this narrative and values struggle is often realized within the context of a larger political struggle between liberal and conservative forces on the frontline of environmental battles. Environmentalists can "use" Native stories and their own narrative perspectives on Native environmental issues to buttress their political arguments, and they are not loath to do so (see, e.g., Dark & MacArthur's, 1996, bibliography of publications by environmentalists on Native American environmentalism).

Moreover, these exotic flavors have seeped into today's media stew. Although Mander (1991) argued that modern media storytelling systems (especially television) are fundamentally anti-Native (and therefore anti-environmental), sectors of the commercial media have had no problem with romanticized visions of the spiritual and natural harmony associated with Native American life. The mass media have occasionally abetted the glorification of Native cultures, focusing predominantly on their "natural religion" and low-impact lifestyle, with the implication that these lifestyles in fact were more "meaningful" than our own lifestyles of consumption and waste. A movie such as *Dances With Wolves*, for instance, portrays Sioux culture as highly harmonized with nature, as well-suited to providing personal and philosophical fulfillment, and superior to White society in every area except perhaps the technical. This movie, an enormous box-office success, arguably does more to shape common knowledge of early cultural practice than all the ethnographies ever written.

Mander argued that this co-optation of romantic aspects of Native life is actually a kind of exploitation of Natives because it separates their art and culture from other aspects of their life that are equally integral. This suggests that the pervasive appropriation of Native stories for environmentalist purposes is a somewhat less-than-honest attempt to use aspects of Native American culture for what are eminently Western political purposes: the purveyance of an environmentalist ideology that attempts to link notions of harmony and stasis to a technologized future.

Modern revisitations of religions such as "Wicca" or "Goddess" ritual also reflect what we see as the wistful belief that older cultures knew more about their environment, often proposing a direct analogy between the Earth and motherhood (Eisler, 1987). But these reflect current cultural needs as much as historical wisdom. Plainly put, they make good stories. Attempts to recover other "ancient ways" are now extremely common in intellectual centers around the United States, often tightly connected with environmental movements. "New Age" movements have attempted to bring down the dominant Western tendencies toward linear, technological thinking, replacing them with holism and self-knowledge. Although these movements vary widely in their intellectual sources, part of their heritage is eastern mysticism, especially certain forms of Buddhism and Taoism.

Although we claim no special expertise in nor animus against New Age philosophies, we note the media emergence of this phenomenon with some interest. Paradoxically, the New Age movement has spawned any number of capitalistic ventures that exploit the apparent commercial appeal of primitive simplicity. These include catalogues such as the Cambridge, Massachusetts-based Earth Star, serving as a clearinghouse for practices as varied as aromatherapy, astrological consulting, "awareness", crystals and minerals, harmonious interior design, healing services, nontraditional medicines, New Age counseling, colon hydrotherapy, retreats, seminars and encounters with mystics, seers, yogis, priests, shamans, and visionaries of various origins. One individual, for instance, offered services as varied as "performing artist, healing

artist, teacher, visionary, poet, ritual maker, and psychic midwife,"
specializing in "polarity process-oriented bodywork, CranioSacral
Therapy, therapeutic massage, authentic movement, and ritual
healing groups for women."

The commonality in all of these approaches is that they
oppose "Western Culture" in some significant way, manifesting a
significant dissatisfaction with technical advancement and mass
society. Yet, at the same time, these philosophies are more and
more committed to spreading their message through technological
means (i.e., the media) and in commercializing their messages.
Each of these philosophies, in their current manifestations, tells us
that we can divest ourselves of trappings and goods and revisit and
relearn ancient ways, while at the same time acquiring goods such
as crystals, Native American art, New Age music tapes, and so on,
to achieve enlightenment. We should acknowledge the polemical
power accruing to these arguments, especially insofar as environmental rhetoric is now beginning to reflect as "received wisdom" the
idea that primitive people actually did live in better harmony with
their environment. Although we do not criticize those who orient
their beliefs in this way, we note the tension that is created when
"primitive" messages are carried in "modern" channels.

As such, our contemporary interpretations, and the activities of modern New Age popularizers, may well obscure the actual
impact primitive or premodern mythologies exerted on environmental conceptions of the audience for such stories. Contrary to popular belief, for instance, many Native American cultures significantly
altered their environment. The modern mythology of the "noble sav-
age" is as much a construction of dissatisfaction with our own
problems as it is a realistic description of any particular ancient
culture. The first obvious problem is the massive generalization
being made about such cultures, which differ as much from each
other in many respects as India differs from China, or the United
States differs from Switzerland. There is also a certain amount of
political correctness in accepting the doctrine that primal cultures
were closer to nature and therefore more harmoniously adapted to
it. Lewis (1992) argued, for instance, that "so-called primal peoples
were not as a rule fully adapted to their environments and did not
exemplify true social harmony. Their societies, like those organized
at a larger scale, have proved capable of the full range of human
good and evil" (p. 55). Lewis cited the evidence of the Rock Cree, a
native North American tribe:

> According to Brightman (1987), the Rock Cree historically not
> only lacked a conservation ethos, but evidently had a "proclivity

to kill animals indiscriminately in number beyond what was needed for exchange of domestic use." In fact, their religious consideration of animals' spirits led not to a conserving respect for nature, but rather to utterly unnecessary destruction. Evidently, members of this group believed that "game killed by hunters [would] spontaneously regenerate after death or reincarnate as fetal animals"; in other words, the more animals were killed, the more the species as a whole would increase. (p. 131)

Thus, not every Native American or traditional culture should be held up as a model for modern environmental policymaking.

On the other hand, misappropriation and monolithic stereotyping of Native stories should not blind us to characteristics they had that may have actually encouraged a closer knowledge of the environment. Certainly, the essential distinction between small-scale societies and large-scale civilizations in the extent to which they pollute cannot be ignored. Although an apparently simple argument is that primal cultures did not pollute because they lacked the technology to do so, it is easy to ignore that the tendency to develop such technology in the West was also part of cultural developments that in fact preceded the actual technological achievements. Because the philosophical and cultural achievements of the Classical world laid the foundation for later technical achievements of Western society, we cannot completely rely on a technological determinism to explain away important relationships between culture, mythology, and environmental attitudes and practice. Part of the primitive failure to pollute, at least in some cases, must have been due to cultural attitudes, lifeways, and stories.

COMMUNICATION FORMS AND THEIR ROLE IN THE ENVIRONMENT

We have a tendency to assume that technological developments play a primary role in the emergence of pollution problems; we pay less attention to the emergence of forms of communication that have also affected the environment. But communication types and patterns have also evolved historically, playing an important role in the emergence and maintenance of environmental problems. There is a sort of "evolution" in communication types and patterns that can be connected to environmental issues. This evolution is certainly not a linear process, but we can document a development in communication types and forms that can then be connected to an understanding of the role played by communication in today's environmental problems.

One hypothesis is that evolving complexity in social organization has produced communication forms that distance people from Nature. Pearce (1989) provided a helpful framework for examining this issue. In his view, communication exists to do three things: coordinate social action, achieve coherence (i.e., meaning), and demonstrate "mystery." Each of these is present in any given cultural enactment of communication. Pearce argued that those societies that we call *primitive* are characterized by *monocultural communication*. This is a kind of communication in which only the ways of communication of the native culture are known or understood. Contact with other cultures is limited or nonexistent, so natives do not make attempts to experience the communication practices of others as being relevant.

Pearce said that "psychological," "sociological," and "cosmological" questions are not differentiated in such a communication practice. "Who" a person is (the psychological question) is closely connected to "what" the society is (the sociological question). More importantly for our purposes, the nature of the world and the universe (the cosmological question) is strongly connected to the individual and social questions. Experiencing stories from communication systems that "link" all aspects of the world in this way should cause the individual to feel as integrally linked to the environment as to oneself or to the culture. That is, self, society, and the world would be seen as a unified "whole." Coordination in such cultures is achieved through a set of common stories (Pearce, n.d.).

In monocultural communication, personal "identity" is derived from relationships to the group and the world. With Pearce, we also hypothesize that stories (*resources*, as Pearce called them) are the communication technologies that tend to conflate individual identities with social and cosmological identities. *Identification* can be defined as the extent to which an individual acknowledges attributes of a phenomenon as defining personhood. Monocultural communication is likely to produce a general congruence between individual, social, and environmental identifications. But monocultural communication forms do not "guarantee" their environmental content. Thus, within a monocultural communication structure, there can be cultures that engage in environmentally destructive practices, just as there are cultures that engage in war, rape, destruction, crime, and a variety of other violent social practices. Communication holism need not be equated with environmental respect. It is therefore no surprise that we can identify primitive cultures that disrespected or exploited nature, just as we can identify aspects of modern culture where environmental respect is practiced.

Still, although we urge the reader caution in interpreting modern accounts of primal environmentalism, we do think that monocultural communication establishes a necessary although not sufficient condition for the emergence of environmental respect in a culture. Monocultural communication establishes the tight "connection" between the individual and the environment; indeed it constitutes the individual as being "of" the environment. Yet what the culture "does" with that connection seems to be up for grabs.

Let's examine one rather interesting case, the case of the Hopi. The Hopi seem to meet most criteria for the definition of a primitive people: small social scale, low technology, subsistence agriculture, family-/clan-based social patterns. Also, their system of stories and religion is replete with natural images. Clans are usually identified with animals. Corn plays a huge role in rituals, and there is a highly evolved and prescribed set of roles and rites through which individuals pass. These rituals have resisted explication by outside interpreters (Waters, 1963). Many people have cited the Hopi example as a meaningful way to avoid the environmental problems of modernity, with Hopi prophecies forming a particular focus, even reaching the popular culture in movies such as *Koyaanisqaatsi (Earth Out of Balance)*, a movie that depicts the gradual deterioration of the Earth at the hands of modernizing technology. Mander (1991) cited Hopi ways as a particularly moving example of Native harmony with nature.

The Hopi story system is extremely complex, filled with characters representing good and evil, and stories of past incarnations of Hopi culture that failed in some respects, especially religious and environmental. Hopi religion tells the story of their people moving through many worlds and many historico-religious "ages"; often the move from one world to another was caused by a failure to hold and observe the religious principles that were supposed to guide them. In this respect, the religion resembles Judeo-Christian religion with its story of "the Fall," except in the case of the Hopi there were several falls, each leading to a new world incarnation and new religious tasks for the people.

The similarity between Hopi religion and, say, Christianity, ends there, but one may say that an "other-worldly" concept is present in the Hopi religion (as much as in more modern forms of religion). Also, the Hopis did not necessarily see themselves as perfectly in harmony with their natural surroundings. In Hopi religion, as much as in Christianity, one finds the notion of imperfect humans striving to meet certain criteria for success as an important moral constituent.

In Christian religion, an other-worldly focus turned into a virtual separation between Nature and Man, whereas the Hopis seemed to use their set of stories to emphasize the connection. Why? Part of the answer may lie in Pearce's concept of the difference between *monocultural communication* and *ethnocentric communication*. Ethnocentric communication (supposedly characteristic of the time in which Christianity emerged) is the product of a technologically modernizing culture, which Pearce argued is catalyzed by the move from hunter-gatherer practices to agricultural practices (this argument echoes Oelschlager's). Although the hunter-gatherer practices have been overly idealized (Lewis, 1992), Pearce emphasized the difference in communication style and the stories represented by these styles. In ethnocentric communication, where many cultures come into initial contact, there is an emergent separation between psychological, sociological, and cosmological questions. This means that

> there is a sense that the sacred is long ago, high above, or far away from the present, although there are periodic manifestations of the sacred. Ordinary life is somehow an expression of or preparation for a life "beyond" the mundane—whether in mystic union with the "one," periodic rebirth, nirvana, or inclusion in the "Holy City" after the Judgment. (p. 125)

In such a system, the necessary condition for environmental respect is eliminated. Thus, Hopi and Christian religion, although manifesting some similarities, operated within different communication contexts (although we have already noted that the Hopi were an agricultural society; this may confound our interpretation slightly and explain some of the other-worldly tendencies in Hopi religion). These contexts in essence may have suggested different "meanings" for stories that were similar in other respects. Ethnocentric stories seem to separate the individual out as subject, replacing the strict communicative connection between individual and cosmos that would have been present in the Hopi system (a monocultural communication system), regardless of the fact that both systems include other-worldly features.

To illustrate, we use an example from Hopi legends. The story of *Hisatsongoopavi*, a Hopi ruin thought to have been devastated by an earthquake, gives an environmental-religious interpretation to how the village was destroyed (Lomatuway'ma, Lomatuway'ma, & Namingha, 1993). The story is about the residents of a village seeking aid from mythical Water Serpents in altering the agricultural landscape of their village. The plan goes awry, and the Serpents begin to wreak havoc, causing earthquakes in the village. The villagers seek aid from a neighboring town, whose shaman tells them:

"What a wretched bunch you are!" he exclaimed. "You've committed a wrong against the people. You seem bent on destroying
everyone. Why on earth did you plan such a thing?" Every one
of you is bad. You had no business doing this. You think you
know it all. Really, you [are] full of vanity," he chastised them.
"It was your desire to do a great feat and to experiment with
something. You ought to know that you are not to do these
things. This world is supposed to stay the way it was created. It
does not behoove us to alter it any way. (p. 35)

The topic of the story is very similar to the Biblical story of
Sodom and Gomorra, where transgressions against the dominant
social order are punished by widespread destruction. However, for
the Hopis, order is ultimately achieved by negotiation between the
shaman and the serpents producing the disaster, whereas in the
Judeo-Christian story the result is produced by an outside force
virtually unnegotiably (although a few virtuous individuals are
saved). In the Hopi story, correct social practice requires a dialogue
with Nature, who is endowed with "character" such that it can be
persuaded, cajoled, and criticized. The shaman goes to discuss the
situation with the Water Serpents:

"Why did you grant the desires of those evil priests? This quake
is now approaching our village to the northeast. I want you to
stop it. Get away from that altar," he ordered them. "You cannot
grant the desires of the evil leaders while having all the people
entrusted to your care. You've known from way, way, back that
you must not fulfill just any old wish. That was not what you
were instructed to do, especially since you are powerful beings."
(p. 39)

Through dialogue, sacrificial offerings, and simple persuasion, the shaman produces a solution that reinforces environmental order and characterizes "the environment" essentially as members of the social community.

In this example, the content of the story reinforces the
importance of the environment and determines resources that community members may bring into play when environmental issues
are at hand. Moreover, the environment is constructed as having
motives, behaviors, and as participating in a set of community
ethics. But environmental harmony is not the point of the story:
the real point is the violation of community norms requiring respect
for religious principles. The message of the story is as much about
hubris as anything else. Still, that the story imbues the environment with character is important, even if that character has an evil
or "trickster" quality. This shows that "primitive" communication

systems did not universally valorize environment. Perhaps the Hopis more universal tendency toward "characterization" of the environment is what produces our current awareness that primitive communication is more environmentally "sensitive." In comparison, the Sodom and Gomorra story, serving a similar religious purpose, has no role for the environment as actor; it is merely a context for action, and a tool in the hands of the superanthropromorphized God.

The perception of the "reality" of stories in monocultural communication is also important. Trafzer (1993) argued that Native American stories should be seen as actual historical accounts, not just fables.

> Elders say that the stories are "actual representations of actual occurrences," but they are more. The stories represent historical actions that provide a creative spark in life, offering significant meanings and interpretations of human action with each other and with the natural environment. . . . The stories are meant for all time and for all generations, and each time they are told, they offer a creative force that links today with yesterday. Thus, they are not like other historical texts, particularly those of Euroamericans. They are circular, carrying the participants in the stories, the storyteller, and the listeners to a time when the first creative energies emerged on earth. (pp. 474-475)

The issue of circularity in such stories is interesting. Whereas the Western story form emphasizes plot development, mystery, suspense, intrigue, and rational explanation at the end (all characteristic of the Western definition of *narrative*), the Native American story follows this form less often. Circularity of form calls attention to the participation of the listener as subject. Linearity of form emphasizes the bracketing of the story by human agency, and therefore positions the listener as "outside" of the story. Repetition in particular is a device of the Native American story that would be poorly understood in the Western context.

Although the question is an extremely complex one, the formal differences between the two systems of communication (monocultural vs. ethnocentric) do seem to mitigate in favor of ecological "consciousness" in earlier primitive cultures, precisely because of the communicative connection between individual, society, and culture. But we need not assume that ecological "consciousness" automatically guaranteed ecological "respect." What is interesting from the communication perspective is that narrative "styles" can remain relatively similar among primitive cultures with radically different results based on their content. Whereas the Hopi system may encourage what we call *environmental protection*, the Rock Cree example mentioned earlier shows that a religious and narrative connection to the natural world need not result in what we would call an environmental *ethos*. It would perhaps be best to argue that a monocultural communication form is probabilistically more likely to yield an environmental ethos. Although the real evidence on narrative form's causal contribution to environmental ethos is slim, Pearce's construct of ethnocentric communication shows that the narrative connections between self and environment, which may have helped cultures to move in environmentally friendly directions, begin to self-destruct with the communicative separation of the individual and the cosmos in the stories of ethnocentric cultures.

The foregoing examples begin to show the importance of narrative in reflecting and even determining environmental attitudes. The emergence of modern communication (again, see Pearce, 1989), where stories begin to question everything, complicates this question enormously, particularly as storytelling functions are co-opted by institutions with commercial and power purposes.

SYSTEMS FOR EXAMINING NARRATIVE CONTRIBUTIONS TO BELIEFS

Our brief examination of some conclusions from the narrative literature shows that narratives contribute to environmental conceptions. The task of the rest of this book is a more direct examination of that contribution in the modern context.

Our goal is to examine how media systems influence environmental conceptions. Our attempts to do this are informed by cultural indicators theory, which is the branch of media research that examines how media representations reflect and reconstruct the culture within which they are found. The most commonly practiced form of this research is known as cultivation research. Cultivation examines relations between exposure to television (assumed to be the dominant cultural mode of storytelling) and beliefs about the real world. The relations measured are assumed to reflect the extent to which the stories of television cultivate (or shape) our perceptions about the world around us (see Gerbner & Gross, 1976; Gerbner, Gross, Morgan, & Signorielli, 1981; Gerbner et al., 1982; Gerbner et al., 1994; Morgan, 1982, 1987, 1990; Morgan, Alexander, Shanahan, & Harris, 1990; Morgan & Shanahan, 1991a, 1991b, 1992; Morgan, Shanahan & Harris, 1990, for examples of cultivation and cultural indicators work).

These approaches are highly suited for the theorist who privileges the power of narrative in his or her work. The unprecedented dominance of the world's storytelling capacity by a single institution (television) suggests that the importance of narrative in constructing perceptions of the world is greatly magnified. If we are to find "media effects" in the area of the environment, most certainly they will at least partly emerge from the fact that stories are monopolized by commercial concerns with monetary and power gains in view.

We view cultural indicators and cultivation as theories of social control. Although the term *social control* may imply dominance, force, and Fascism, we recognize that every social grouping, every culture, has mechanisms of social control. Therefore, many theories of mass communication have dealt with the issue of social control. Critical and cultural theories have been especially attentive to social control issues. Narrative theories tend to focus less on the issue of control. Cultivation and cultural indicators, however, among the empirical approaches to mass communication, are conceived specifically as both theories of narrative and of social control.

Cultivation theory is concerned with the way television encourages people to think about social order. Why television? With the universal adoption of television, traditional storytellers (the church, family, the schools, even the state) have been challenged by a mass medium that tends to present a commercially produced, more or less homogeneous view of the world. People who are otherwise distinct from one another are addressed as a mass audience, which can then be segmented across demographic variables as marketing needs require. Because television serves this cultural function of message sending and storytelling, it has become the focus of cultivation research. In many ways, television also represents the pinnacle of development from monocultural, to ethnocentric, to modern communication, in that television facilitates the final break in the connection between story and environment. Thus, television's impacts on environmental conceptions may be especially important.

We ground cultivation and cultural indicators research with five propositions. These propositions show how cultivation research approaches and examines social phenomena, in this case, the environment.

Proposition 1 assumes that institutions of mass communication are controlled by social, cultural, and primarily economic elites. Cultivation researchers are most concerned with the aspects of a media system in which ownership and access are limited and tightly controlled. Cultivation researchers have fairly frequently analogized television to institutions such as preindustrial religion to show the extent to which it is perceived as a dominant institution. Who are these elites? Simply put, we refer to corporate elites that dominate media ownership and are increasing and concentrating this dominance. These elites dominate other major sectors of society within the dominant social paradigm, as should be evident.

In Proposition 2, we assume that social and economic elites codify messages in their media to serve elite aims. This proposition is in consonance with much of the narrative theory we have discussed, which is that narratives and their messages are extremely effective tools for creating and maintaining structures of meaning. The ability to contribute to meaning is coextensive with the power to participate in processes of social control.

Proposition 3 proposes that messages in media content can be empirically studied. Empirical study reveals messages that conform to elite needs and desires. The third proposition moves our cultural indicators research to the empirical domain. Although the first two propositions are "assumed," cultural indicators work has had a long tradition of content-analytic research. In particular, the analyses of violent messages and the unequal demographics of television have been compelling in demonstrating the thesis that social elites codify their messages in media content. To assume that social elites also codify preferred environmental messages is not too much of a leap. We test that idea in the next chapter.

Proposition 4 states that audience members, although perhaps seeking to fulfill individual needs, participate in a social process in which they hear and internalize messages of social elites. Cultivation research assumes that massive attention to television results in a slow, steady, and cumulative internalization of aspects of those messages, especially the aspects with ideological import.

This proposition does not necessarily imply that aims of social elites will be universally accepted by viewers (see Proposition 5), but it does suggest that social elites have a resource with which to condition public discussion of social, political, economic, and environmental issues. Thus, cultivation argues that an important outcome of our media system is that social elites can play a disproportionate role in determining the "boundaries" of social discourse. This tilts the field in favor of social elites and predisposes toward an eventual outcome of social control.

Finally, Proposition 5 states that audience members more "committed" to media will have belief structures more consonant with those desired by social elites. This proposition is the one directly tested by cultivation analysis: viewership (i.e., exposure to television) is related to belief structures, under the assumption that more time spent with an elite-dominated media system reflects: (a) a willingness to accept the propositions within those media as "useful," and (b) a tendency to accept propositions within those media as, in some sense, "factual." This proposition states that the internalization processes hypothesized in Proposition 4 will result in outcomes that serve social elites. We test this proposition, with respect to environmental conceptions, in the chapter 5.

In summary, then, cultivation is a theory of social control through mass media. Cultivation theory adopts some propositions from critical theory and adapts them for testing some final propositions, arguing that television messages are a vehicle for social control. Audiences' acceptance of these messages is measured as the congruity between the television worldview and audience belief systems. Data showing congruence between audience beliefs and television messages are functionally interpreted as serving needs and desires of the elites that control messages.

RESEARCH QUESTIONS

The specific research questions examined in the remainder of this book deal with observable relationships between media content and people's environmental perceptions and conceptions. Up to this point we have been concerned with establishing a theoretical basis for examining the importance of narrative for environmental issues. Now, we would argue that a move to empirical observation and analysis is necessary to put our thoughts on a more firm footing. In essence, we argue that the dimensions and effects of narrative should be examined at more than a theoretical level. Our next chapters attempt to do this.

Here we should note that we venture into territory that some see as controversial. Cultural indicators work in particular has been attacked as being sterile because of its attempt to use relatively "standard" techniques of social science to make critical arguments. We stipulate here that, although some may be discouraged by databased explorations of complex social issues, from our perspective, a move to data is simply the logical next step in the analysis we propose. That is, if stories are as powerful as we have suggested, how do these effects manifest themselves?

Thus, in chapter 4 we begin with a 4-year content analysis of television's messages about the environment. This is designed to simply describe the environmental narrative dimensions of today's most powerful medium. It answers the question, "What is being said?". We suggest that the reader think of this as an alternate kind of textual analysis, and as is seen, there is no shortage of interpretation attached to this work. Unlike most studies, which tend to analyze news programs, we examine prime-time entertainment programs. Cultural indicators research normally deals with prime-time programming because it represents the most viewed and important aspect of the television story system. In this chapter, we ask the basic question: "What's on?". Concurrently, we examine what's not on. We examine the role of nature and the environment in more than 400 programs, sampled from the years between 1991 and 1995. These analyses allow us to paint a broad-brush picture of the attention television pays to the natural environment, and what narrative and functional roles are fulfilled by environmental images.

Knowing what is being said, the next concern is how it is being interpreted. Normally in critical research, this is done through a more or less hermeneutical process of textual interpretation. Without criticizing that approach, we adopt a quantitative form of hermeneutics, which examines interpretative tendencies at a more macrosocial level. Thus, in chapter 5, our research question is: "How do images affect viewers?". Using data from National Opinion Research Center surveys and from our own surveys, we perform cultivation analyses of relationships between television viewing and cnvironmental beliefs, attitudes, and knowledge. Again, our focus is on the impacts from viewing prime-time narratives. As is seen, some complex and counterintuitive findings emerge from this analysis.

Then, we turn our attention to a single "story." In chapter 6, we examine a particular narrative from the history of environmental media. The issue of global warming became a focus of environmental hysteria in the media. In this chapter, our research question focuses on the role of "cycles" in constructing environmental narratives such as global warming. Using a content analysis of newspaper coverage of the issue, we examine how journalists and audiences construct narratives of environmentally dangerous phenomena. Again, although we use some techniques of quantification, the goal is to provide a critical interpretation of an environmental story. In that sense, our look at the "myths" being constructed about and around global warming are not unlike the analyses we gave of the "primitive" Hopi story: Its purpose is to examine the social functions and consequences of environmental storytelling.

four

TELEVISION'S
PORTRAYAL OF THE
ENVIRONMENT

In this chapter, we move to an empirical examination of narrative impacts on the environment.[1] Our attempt in this and the following chapters is to provide a general understanding of (a) how the environment is presented in the dominant media narratives of the day, and (b) the effects of those narratives on people's beliefs, knowledge, and concern about the environment. Indeed, if the theory discussed in the previous chapters is valid, we should be able to observe and measure relationships between the consumption of environmental narratives and what people think about nature.

But, of course, "quantifying" narratives is a rather difficult task. A narrative is a very human construct. Getting even a few people to agree about what the components, messages, characters, and morals of narratives are can be difficult. The narrative one person sees as providing meaningful lessons about nature may be seen by another as being about an entirely different topic. So any

[1]The first 2 years of data were reported in Shanahan (1996). The full 4-year sample is reported in *Journalism and Mass Communication Quarterly* (Shanahan & McComas, 1997). This chapter is based on those analyses, with more extensive reporting, review, and analysis of data. Also, additional discussions are presented.

quantification procedure, no matter how well designed and execut-
ed, can be misleading or biased. Similarly, any attempt to quantify
people's reactions to narratives can be misleading or biased.
Certainly survey research procedures can gloss over important
individual differences, just as content analysis can obscure the
meanings and import of individual narratives.

So why do it? A few answers are relevant. First, we again
emphasize that the purpose of this book is to examine narrative
systems as much as possible, and we feel that can only be done at
the broader level facilitated by quantitative analysis. With the widespread dissemination of environmental narratives and their widespread reception, it seems vital to understand at the broadest possible level how these processes work. Also, as our literature review
has shown, many more studies have done the work of looking at
individual pieces of the environmental story; our attempt to look at
the bigger picture is intended to complement that aspect of the literature. A second answer is that any process of human interpretation is subjective, reflecting biases, choices of presentation, political
ideology, and so on. And we recognize that the quantifying procedures of social science are just as open to bias as any other form of
interpretation. We see social science procedures as simply another
way to interpret human phenomena, and in particular, they offer a
somewhat more replicable way to analyze relationships between
narratives and beliefs. Readers can reach their own interpretations
about environmental narratives armed with same data as we use.
So we offer the next few chapters in the spirit of the theory that has
gone beforehand. That is, as an experiment in critical empiricism,
we attempt to see the extent to which our critical ideological position can be substantiated by hopefully somewhat dispassionate
observation and measurement.

McKibben (1992), the well-known environmental writer,
argued that modern culture erodes our knowledge of environmental
issues. He asserted that television takes away from environmental
knowledge because it dominates our consciousness to an unprecedented extent:

> We believe that we live in the "age of information," that there
> has been an information "explosion," an information "revolu-
> tion." While in a certain narrow sense this is the case, in many
> important ways just the opposite is true. We also live at a
> moment of deep ignorance, when vital knowledge that humans
> have always possessed about who we are and where we live
> seems beyond our reach. An Unenlightenment. An age of miss-
> ing information. (p. 9)

For McKibben, a comparison of what one might learn from a day's worth of television programs and what one might learn from a day in the Adirondacks was meant to illustrate the boundaries and dimensions of the disappearing information. The implication was that television's pervasive and studious inattention to the environment results in societal neglect of environmental issues and a historically unprecedented loss of experience with and knowledge of the natural world. His argument resonates very strongly with our own perspective on the role of television in facing environmental issues. Especially because television is institutionally geared to serve a consumerist society in which the dominant social paradigm continues to thrive, we see television as playing a specifically anti-environmental role.

But does television "ignore" the environment? McKibben did not "content analyze" the television programs he discussed; he reported his perspective on their salient aspects. In this chapter, we examine patterns of television "coverage" of environmental issues, looking at the years 1991 through 1995. Focusing on prime-time televised entertainment, we examine how the issue of the environment appears in the "background" of televised culture, both through an analysis of nature as a "theme" in television entertainment and through an analysis of "episodes" within programs which have explicit environmental content.

MESSAGE SYSTEMS

Cultural indicators research normally examines message systems, an approach different from many research approaches that examine specific media programs, campaigns, and/or information. In order to assess broad-based social impacts of messages, cultural indicators research prefers to examine the types and categories of messages that are repeated and reinforced in cultural narratives. Signorielli and Morgan (1990) noted that the purpose of message system analysis is "identifying and assessing the most recurrent and stable patterns of television content (the consistent images, portrayals, and values that cut across most types of programs)" (p. 19). What remains the same in television content is seen as influencing and reflecting our broad social conceptions.

Images from specific programs reflect changing cultural currents, trends, and fads, while the stability of the message system reflects the mainstream within which those currents diverge. Although specific messages may have impacts of their own, our analysis is designed to reveal broad program trends and characteristics. As we saw in chapter 2, some programs and information campaigns have documented effects on their audiences (e.g., exposure to Cousteau programs was seen to have some ephemeral knowledge effects; Fortner & Lyon, 1985), whereas a variety of studies showed that information campaigns could increase the "salience" of environmental knowledge; Griffin, 1989, 1990). But, overall, the research has shown that these impacts tend to be minimal, ephemeral, and more focused on environmental attitude (as opposed to behavior). If anything, the lesson of the existing literature is that changes and effects due to specific programs are difficult to detect (a point we raised when discussing Hansen's, 1991, work). Perhaps failure to detect effects from specific programs may simply indicate that we need to look at a different level.

Cultural indicators' concern with message systems can also be connected to our earlier discussion of narrative. With Barthes (1957), cultural indicators research sees the invariant features of television narrative as establishing "commonsense" boundaries for belief, discourse, and ideology. With Burke (1945), cultural indicators sees the invariant "background" images as establishing a "scene" within which individually variant actions and plotlines take place; such a scene implies and legitimates the actions that take place within it. We see the consistent features of the message system as reflecting the social environment discussed in chapter 2: the deeper cultural and narrative interpretation of the environment that is constituted and reconstituted in our narrative systems.

RESEARCH QUESTIONS

It is somewhat surprising that prime-time television programs have not been more frequently content analyzed for environmental issues (especially because they have so frequently been analyzed for other themes). One factor militating against this is that news is typically seen as the appropriate channel for environmental content, because environmentalism has been seen primarily as a sociopolitical "issue." Thus, newspaper and broadcast journalism coverage has been more frequently examined.

Yet, although news may "use" narratives to present information, most of the other programs on television are narratives, with no pretense of providing information. Still, such programs do present information, and we know that this information is retained by audiences (Gerbner & Gross, 1976). We explore the boundaries of information retained by audiences in chapter 5, but here we can note that environmental narratives found in entertainment programs are potentially, from an educational standpoint, just as socially important (and perhaps more so) than those presented in news, especially because viewers of entertainment are much less prepared to erect defenses against the information they may glean from their leisure-time viewing.

Because our studies are among the first to examine environmental content in entertainment programming, they are essentially descriptive and exploratory. Our goal is to find out how frequently the environment appears as a theme in prime-time programs, and how often specific environmental issues come up in such programs. We assumed, along with McKibben (1992), that "attention" to environmental issues would be low, but we hoped to be able to sample enough episodes dealing with environmental issues to describe television's "background portrayal" of the environment.

We were also interested in detecting trends in media attention to the environment in the 4 years of our sample. Our sampling began in 1991, a period of relatively close social attention to environmental issues, and ended in 1995, when such attention had declined perceptibly. It is of some interest to know whether television's attention to environmental issues follows the general opinion climate. Although it is unlikely that television entertainment programs "drive" public attention to issues such as the environment, it seems more reasonable that such attention is a barometer of the extent to which an issue "penetrates" the deeper cultural consciousness. We hypothesized that television's attention to environmental issues would decline from 1991 to 1995 because we felt that television's attention to environmental issues reflected a shallower "trend" in issue awareness, as opposed to a real paradigmatic change in cultural-environmental commitment.

We were also interested in some other characteristics of environmental content in prime-time television. We gathered data about TV "characters" connected to environmental episodes and their characteristics. Characters were individuals narratively associated with environmental issues in programs. The information we gathered focused mostly on demographic characteristics of the characters associated with environmental episodes in television: race, gender, SES, occupation, and so on.

We were also interested in being able to provide a narrative "overview" of environmental episodes seen on television. Thus, after analyzing our quantitative content data, we move to a more interpretive analysis of the environmental episodes we coded, looking at the episodes in their narrative context. Finally, we provide some descriptive quantitative information of environmental presentations in news and advertising.

METHODS

This chapter extends and follows the method presented in earlier studies (Shanahan, 1992, 1996). In three randomly chosen week-long time periods (November 1991; January 1993; and February 1994) all programs appearing on the three Boston network affiliates were recorded from the access and prime-time slot (7 p.m.-11 p.m.). In September through October 1995, all such programs were taped from the Ithaca area affiliates in Syracuse and Binghamton, New York. All programs appearing on the local network affiliate were analyzed, even if they were not network programs (although most were network programs). The sample included network news programs, local feature/magazine programming, local news programming, syndicated first-run programming, and regular network entertainment (including some "off-network" syndication). Four hours of programming were sampled on three networks on seven evenings in the 4-week samples, yielding 336 potential hours of sample content. Due to some technical problems in the 1994 sample, we coded 317 of these hours, in 402 separate programs.[2]

We looked at each program using a four-part coding instrument. The first part was based on the content coding scheme long used in cultural indicators research to record basic information about the themes appearing in programs. The various themes (there were 16) included "relationships between the genders," "media/entertainment," "law enforcement/crime," "health," "science," and so forth. A theme for "nature," also used in the cultural indicators coding scheme, was included. The coding scheme employed allowed for themes to be coded as "absent," representing a "minor" focus, representing a "secondary" focus, or representing a "primary" focus of a program. This section of the coding instrument also included items measuring basic information about the program (time, network, genre, etc.).

---

[2]We assumed that the number of programs dealing with environmental issues at all would be relatively small, perhaps around 10% of the total. To detect a population proportion of 10% (with a .05 margin of error) in a universe of 4,329 programs (a yearly estimate computed by multiplying the number of programs in our sample 1995 week by 39, leaving out 13 weeks for a summer season) requires a sample of about 140 programs (Scheaffer, Mendenhall, & Ott, 1990). Because we sampled only 1 week's worth of programming in each year, it turned out that our yearly samples were below that number (our average sample size was 100.5 programs). Thus, our yearly estimates should be interpreted with caution. The combined 4-year data set, with 402 programs, is sufficiently large to detect effects of any size, so our aggregated data analyses can be generalized more successfully.

The first section also recorded the number of environmental "episodes" appearing in each program. An environmental episode was defined as any discrete portion of a program involving spoken words or physical action in which environmental issues were specifically implicated or discussed. That is, we coded any episode with a meaningful environmental position in the narrative of the program. Environmental "images" and background scenery were more difficult to code, since almost any image could be given an environmental interpretation, so we did not code them.

Episodes were coded as either environmentally "concerned," "neutral," or "unconcerned." Concerned episodes were those that expressed approval of the importance of environmental issues or implicitly supported environmental positions. For instance, if a character in a sitcom mentioned recycling and either explicitly or implicitly supported it, that would be a concerned episode. Neutral episodes took no position but mentioned the environment. Unconcerned episodes were those where specific opposition was taken to environmental issues or where such opposition was implicated. In some cases, for instance, environmental issues became the focus of a joke or putdown. Criticizing someone as a "tree-hugger" would be an example of an unconcerned environmental episode.

The next part of the instrument coded details about the episode. Demographic information about who performed the episode was coded. For each environmental episode, we coded information about what specific environmental issues were discussed or implicated. Thus, each episode can be described as being specifically about certain issues, including acid rain, global warming, toxic waste, and so forth.[3]

RESULTS

Prevalence of Nature as Theme in Television Programs

Overall, we found that the nature theme appears relatively infrequently in television programs. To count as a theme, natural or

---

[3]Data were coded by the authors; some assistants were used at various points throughout the sample span. Coding pretests and extensive coder training were done to enhance intercoder reliability prior to recording the data in each of the four separate years. In order to more accurately assess coder reliability, we double coded a 15% subsample of the 1995 data. We analyzed coder reliability in the assessment of program themes, and found, using Scott's pi as an estimate, an intercoder reliability of .69. This figure is extremely close to the minimum bound of .70 suggested by Singletary (1994).

environmental issues had to be a narrative part of the program. Simple scenic backgrounds of trees, for instance, did not count. However, a narratively important natural setting for a program, such as the wilderness or mountains, did establish nature as a theme in a program.

Nature is completely absent as a theme, using our judgment criteria, in almost 80% of programming, and it is an outstanding theme in only 1.7% of the 402 programs we coded. Compared to other themes such as media/entertainment, family, personal relationships, and financial success, nature as a theme is very infrequent. For instance, the relationship theme is paramount in 23.4% of all programs, whereas the family theme is primary in 31.2% of all sampled programs.

This is not too unexpected a finding, which McKibben (1992) highlighted. Television draws attention to the human world and is itself a human-created environment. So it is not surprising that human-centered themes have dominated the narrative world of TV. Table 4.1 shows frequency of appearance for selected themes in prime-time television.

However, nature is by no means the only marginalized theme. For instance, religion was the primary theme in only one of the programs we sampled, and it was absent as a theme from more than 85% of our sample. If nature and religion often go together in our thinking (McKibben, 1994), then it is perhaps more than coincidence that television tends to ignore both.[4]

Of course, the frequency of appearance of nature as a theme tends to vary with program genre. Figure 4.1 shows the prevalence of nature as more than an incidental theme in selected genres. What is surprising is that nature appears as a theme most frequently in action-adventure and reality-show genres. Even more than news (where one expects to see environmental issues), these shows often have content and backgrounds that suggest that nature is, for them, a somewhat important theme. Action-adventure shows such as *Baywatch* and *Jake and the Fatman* are one type. In programs such as these, nature often serves as a "test" for heroic individuals (see chapter 3). In reality shows such as *Rescue 911*, it is again nature that often presents the test for heroic individuals (and their sheltering institutions) to excel: floods, forest

---

[4]We might note that more recent programs, such as *Touched by an Angel*, are introducing a much heralded return to religious themes on TV. Such programs, however, could just as easily be coded using our supernatural theme. Hollywood, pleased with the success of the angel theme, is introducing other programs to capitalize on this fad. With millenial hype building at this writing, it would be safe to say that religious themes might get deeper treatment in the next few years.

Table 4.1. Relative Frequency of Appearance of Selected Themes in Prime-Time Programs.

Theme ->	Nature (%)	Religion (%)	Personal Relation-ships (%)	Family (%)	Media/ Entertain-ment (%)	Financial Success Money (%)
Theme is absent	78.9	85.5	38.6	26.2	52.9	56.9
Theme is minor	11.4	11.5	17.2	20.0	13.7	17.2
Theme is secondary	8.0	2.7	20.9	22.7	12.2	10.2
Theme is primary	1.7	.2	23.4	21.2	21.2	15.7

Note. Nature and religion themes are positively correlated (Spearman correlation = .13; $p < .01$). Nature and relationship themes are negatively correlated (Spearman correlation = -.13; $p < .05$).

fires, earthquakes, and so on, all represent Mother Nature at her angriest, testing Man's resolve. These programs teach us to respect that nature can test us in her most powerful moments, but that we can overcome with resolve and courage.

In other genres, nature was not as important. In particular, the "inward-directed" type of program (e.g., a sitcom) tends to ignore natural themes. As Barnouw noted (1970), the television drama or comedy, much like the Ibsen drama, draws the viewer "inside" so as to deal with themes interior to the human mental experience.

To examine how nature relates to other themes on television, we conducted a multidimensional scaling analysis using 10 of the themes we coded (Norusis, 1993). This analysis uses ratings of the dissimilarities between themes' importance in programs to characterize the overall "spatial" relationship among them in the body of programs. This tells us whether, for instance, nature generally does not appear as a theme when family themes are present, or whether money and personal relationship themes tend to "go together." The scaling analysis produces "dimensions" that visually map the themes in relation to each other.

Our analysis, presented in Figure 4.2, shows that nature themes tend to be very separate from themes such as personal relationships, family, law/crime, and the money/entertainment themes. Thus, not only are nature themes less frequent, but they are conceptually separate from the numerically dominant themes in prime time. Although not unexpected, this analysis highlights that nature themes are not considered important in television programs that explore the human-centered themes dominating programming.

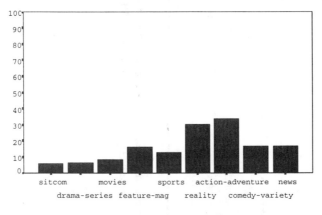

Figure 4.1. Percentage of programs with nature as more than minor theme, by genre

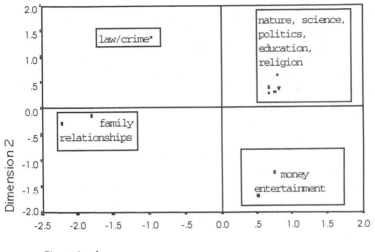

Figure 4.2. Multidimensional scaling analysis of 10 themes in prime-time programs
Note. Stress = .16, R^2 = .92

On the other hand, nature themes are very close to politics, science, religion, and education. Of all the themes tested in our study, nature is conceptually closest to religion. We think this shows that nature, like politics, religion, and so forth, is considered an "issue," whereas the dominant themes such as personal relationships, entertainment, and others are not issues but aspects of "lifestyle." That is, nature, religion, politics, and so on, are subjects that are appropriately thought of in rational terms using "facts" and "information." Because TV narratives generally favor presentations dealing with more entertainment-oriented themes, the environment is marginalized somewhat. The fact that television programs apparently make a very distinct separation between issues and lifestyles is of great significance for the environment, especially if viewers make a similar separation in their own minds (which we explore somewhat in chapter 5).

Although it is not surprising that television entertainment programs are not more environmentally focused, it is perhaps more intriguing to note that the frequency and importance of the appearance of nature as a theme has declined in recent years. Figure 4.3 shows how the overall importance of the nature theme in programs has declined from a high point in the first year of our sample and dropped off drastically in 1995. This analysis is computed by averaging the scale values for the nature theme in all programs, ranging from 0 (*theme is absent*) to 3 (*theme is primary*). All themes tend to vary in importance from year to year in our sample, but the nature theme is the only one that shows a monotonic decrease (test for linearity: $F = 9.18$; $p = .0026$). This analysis supports the hypothesis that narrative attention to environmental issues has slipped in recent years, perhaps because of an overall decline in social attention to environmental issues.

Given this, it is difficult to conclude that television's attention to environmental issues reflects any sort of paradigmatic or cultural change. Rather, we hypothesize that television's attention reflects cyclical peaks in awareness of the environment. Thus, the relatively high value for the early years in our sample corresponds to a higher level awareness for the culture in general. As that awareness and excitement dipped, so did television's attention.

Setting

Earlier we argued that the concept of *place* is important to an understanding of how environmental narratives work. In accord with this view, we think that the *setting* of television programs conveys a good deal of information about the environmental conceptions inherent in the television message system. To determine the scene of television narratives requires at least some basic information about the location and setting of programs. We coded programs for a few variables to determine the scene of action.

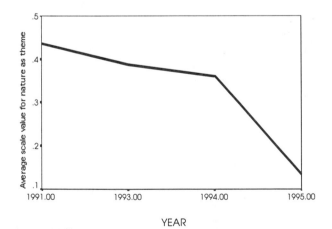

Figure 4.3. Prevalence of nature as theme in programs, by year
Note. 1 = theme is absent, 3 = theme is primary
Test of linearity: F = 9.1878; p < .0026

Table 4.2 shows how many programs were set in urban, small-town, and rural locales. It is evident that the vast majority of programs in prime time—almost 95%—are primarily set in urban locales (however, it should be noted that a good many programs were difficult to code, due to extremely mixed settings; news programs were difficult to code, for instance). Comparing these data to household figures available from the 1990 U.S. census shows that the TV universe tends to overestimate the number of people living in urban locales (approximately 75%). The tendency of television to overfocus on human-created, urban environments is rather striking.

It may be concluded from this that lifestyles that are more "connected" (assuming that an urban lifestyle is somewhat more disconnected from environmental experience) to the environment tend to be underrepresented. Farm families, for instance, hardly appear at all in our sample of fictional programs. We see in our analysis of character demographics that the professions and qualities of characters associated with environmental episodes also match this phenomenon.

Also, television programs tend to take the viewer inside. We found that a plurality of programs are shot entirely in studio locations. A majority are shot either entirely or mostly in the studio. Programs that spend more of their time outside the studio are relatively rare. It is important to note that we counted the narrative location, not the actual location. That is, programs that may have used studio settings to simulate the outdoors were counted as outdoors.

Although we recognize that in-studio taping is less expensive, it is striking that so many programs are confined to indoor locations. In combination with the previous analysis, the extent to which television moves the viewer into an interior world is of some consequence (see Figure 4.4). The tendency is particularly notice-

Table 4.2. Setting of Television Programs.

	Television Data (%)		Census Data (%)
Urban	79.1	urban—inside urbanized area	62.8
Small town	14.7	urban—outside urbanized area	11.7
Rural	3.3	rural	25.4
Uninhabited	.4		
"Mobile"	2.6		

Note. Television programs that had mixed settings, or could not otherwise be coded for setting, are not included in this table. Census data are obtained from U.S. census data lookup service (http://venus.census.gov/CD-ROM/lookup).

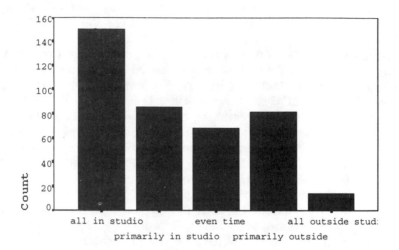

Figure 4.4. "Location" of television programs: Inside studio vs. outside studio

able in the bread-and-butter genres such as sitcoms, where almost everything occurs within a single room or house. The "family" in the family show is thus often constructed as limited to a particular space, a "haven in a heartless world" (Lasch, 1975). The implications for conceptions of nature are important. As Lasch noted: "The withdrawal into the 'emotional fortress' of the family took place not because family life became warmer and more attractive in the nineteenth century, . . . but because the outside world came to be seen as more forbidding" (p. 168). Lasch's analysis suggests that the popularity of the sitcom and teledrama have something to do with the escapism they provide from the challenging and dangerous "outside" world.

Episodes

Our analysis of environmental episodes allows for a closer look at the environmental content of television programs. We should note that such episodes occur relatively infrequently, even in programs that have nature as a theme. A show that could have nature as an important backdrop theme (think of a movie such as *Cliffhanger*, shot entirely in a natural setting) might have no explicit codeable references to environmental issues yielding an environmental episode. Figure 4.5 shows that the absolute frequency of such

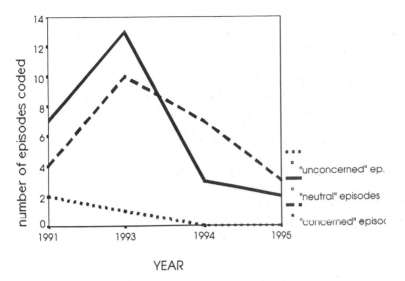

YEAR

Figure 4.5. Number of environmental "episodes," by type and year

episodes has declined markedly since 1993. Although the 1994 sample is somewhat smaller (partially explaining the decrease in that year), the overall pattern is one of marked decline of explicit references to environmental issues. When such episodes appear, however, they do appear either to "support" the environment or at least take a neutral position. Because the number of environmental episodes in each year's sample is low, we did not calculate statistical significances for the observed trends; the numbers are purely descriptive.

Our analysis shows, as the previous thematic analysis did, that nature and environmental portrayals are more likely when the issue of environmentalism is more prominent. That is, when sociopolitical aspects of environmental issues are higher on the issue agenda, it is also more likely that popular culture programs will focus on the environment. The corollary to this is that such attention will rapidly disappear when the social and political attention fades. Our data imply that the environment appears to be cyclically foregrounded, then marginalized in televised culture.

When environmental episodes appear, it is interesting to know what they were about, so as to make a judgment about what issues are being presented to public opinion through the medium of prime-time television. In the environmental episodes we coded, the most frequently appearing single issue dealt with particular species of animals and species protection (see Figure 4.6). This is because animals are sometimes characters in TV shows, and because species protection is a proven attractive issue for television audiences (think of classic programs such as *Wild Kingdom, Jacques Cousteau,* and *National Geographic*). Also, obviously, we have a certain tendency to anthropromorphize animals to reflect human concerns. Water and air pollution were also important foci for television environmental episodes. Interestingly, environmental activism was also a frequently appearing issue, as characters in comedies and dramas either portrayed or commented on the characteristics and qualities of the environmental activist. Often, activism was the focus of a joke. Again, it should be noted that all of these issues appeared in episodes occurring relatively infrequently. However, coming as they do from our aggregated 4-year sample, we may interpret them as representative of what an average viewer could see in a given week of prime-time television.

Demography of Environmental Episodes. For each episode we analyzed, we collected data on the character who "performed" the episode. In our coding scheme, this was the character who carried the narrative action of the episode. Normally, this was a fairly easy identification to make, because a single character generally spoke or made a proposition that constituted the episode. In a few cases, deciding which character to identify as the performer was more difficult. In these cases, we made subjective decisions.

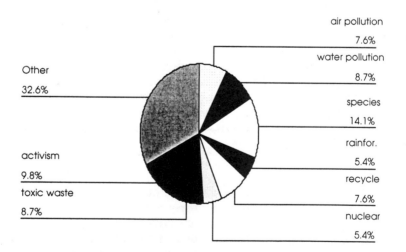

Figure 4.6. Distribution of issue foci in environmental episodes observed in fictional and entertainment-oriented programs

For each character coded demographic features were described. These variables included race, gender, age, nationality, SES, and occupation. Taken together, these variables allow us to provide a demography of television environmentalism: that is, when environment is the topic, who speaks?

Table 4.3 presents a summary of this information. First, we see that characters performing environmental episodes on programs tend to be male, by about a 2 to 1 margin. Although this may suggest that Hollywood and network programmers put the environmental issue ball in males' hands, we should recall that male characters outnumber females throughout television by about the same margin (Signorielli & Morgan, 1990). Still, with environmentalism often proclaimed to be a "woman's issue," it is surprising and instructive that the difference is so great.

The racial makeup of characters performing environmental episodes also closely mirrors the general TV program demography. Blacks generally comprise about 12% to 13% of TV program characters, with Whites dominating and "other" races filling in the gaps. Our sample reveals environmental episodes occurred both in "Black" shows (such as *Cosby* or the *Royal Family*) and in White shows (such as *Coach* or *Cybil*) with a frequency proportional to that seen in TV demography and in the real world.

The SES of characters performing environmental episodes skews toward the upper end of the spectrum. Very few "lower class" characters were seen or heard discussing environmental issues in their programs (although we should again note that there are fewer such characters in programs overall). Most characters were either middle class (58.7%) or upper class (39.1%). Perhaps this is not too surprising considering that environmentalism itself has been perceived as an upper class, privileged social movement. Recent developments in "environmental justice" notwithstanding, television does not present environmental issues in the context of lower and working-class concerns.

Finally, we examined the occupation of characters performing environmental episodes. We found, somewhat surprisingly, that a plurality of such characters were involved in "entertainment" occupations. In some cases, these were hosts of entertainment programs such as *Jeopardy* and did not "narratively" espouse environmental views.[5] In other cases, the characters were narratively portrayed in entertainment roles, such as football coach.

Again, perhaps surprisingly, "business" was the next leading occupation of characters performing environmental episodes.

---

[5]*Jeopardy*, although not a fictional program, was coded as entertainment rather than news.

Table 4.3. "Demography" of Environmental Episodes.

	Gender		**Age**		**Race**
Percent male	64.7%	Percent adolescent	11.8%	Percent white	82.7%
Percent female	35.3%	Percent "young adult"	29.4%	Percent black	11.5%
		Percent "middle-aged"	52.9%	Percent other	5.8%
		Percent elderly	5.9%		

	Nationality		**SES**		**Occupation**
Percent U.S.	98%	Percent "lower class"	2.8%	Percent entertainment	40.4%
Percent foreign	2%	percent "middle class"	58.7%	Percent business	21.3%
		Percent "upper class"	39.1%	Percent government	10.6%
				Percent education	14.9%

As is seen in our analysis of news stories, environmental issues (when they were presented) are very often connected to business issues in television programs. Although characters involved in business as an occupation need not have brought a business context to bear on the environmental episode, it does reflect the general pro-DSP ideology that television uses to discuss environmental issues. We discuss this issue in more detail latter.

These demographic descriptions (along with some other figures provided in Table 4.3) give a general picture of "who" presents environmental issues. Taken together with the previous discussion, they show some of the outlines of television's message system for environmental issues.

Episodes in Narrative Context. As we have seen, few environmental episodes occurred in our programs (compared to violent events, for instance, which occur six to eight times per hour). Although a statistical examination of these episodes is useful, a narrative examination of their content is also important because it places the episodes in a context that viewers would actually use to understand them. Moreover, it helps narratively to get a sense of how the episodes fit in programs: whether they are "important," whether they are treated humorously or seriously, and so on. In this section, we give brief descriptions of how environmental episodes fitted into the overall narrative structure of the programs that contained them.

First let's look at the 1991 sample. One "environmentally concerned" event was encountered in the ABC program *Step by Step*, in which an adolescent male character commented on the natural beauty of a location in which the family was camping. Specific mention was made of the lack of cars and how "this is the life." This particular episode is typical of many of the environmental episodes that we coded: They were mostly apolitical and praised the beauty of the natural environment in comparison to the drudgery of city life. This kind of concern can be considered typical of one form of network presentation of environmentalism: It "supports" the basic idea of beauty, wilderness, and nature; the "environment" is also constructed as being separate from the context of "normal" life, which is the city.

In the NBC program *Sisters*, there was a dispute between neighbors about a tree on the border of their property. One neighbor demands that the tree be chopped down and complains about having so many trees around (they interfere with his use of the property). The fact that he complains about trees is meant to show that he is a crotchety crank. The protagonist says that "trees are beautiful" and defends the right of the tree to exist. Here, we have two environmental episodes, one concerned and one unconcerned, although again the level of "politicization" on the issue is minimal. In fact, the tree dispute becomes a dramatic device used to introduce a later resolution in which we find out that the mean-old-tree-hater is really lonely because of the recent death of his wife. He eventually saves the tree-lovers' son who falls out of the tree while playing. There is a happy ending as the neighbors get together for a friendly dinner. The tree stays. This episode appropriates nature symbolism to make a dramatic point: The tree is a symbol of life that eventually unites the quarreling neighbors.

An episode of *Designing Women* contained a section in which a character expressed anti-hunting views. This was coded as a concerned episode, although many hunters consider themselves environmentalists. Another character responded to her in a separately coded event that hunting was necessary to keep the deer population down. The general thrust of the interchange was comedic rather than informational because the point was to portray one of the characters as a macho rural rube, in opposition to the enlightened urban stance of the protagonist. Here, environmentalism and "anti-environmentalism" were used to help define character types: Clearly the program producers saw these as stock characters with predictable attitudes that could be used to dramatic effect. The overall episode, promoting the "humanity" of the deer preservation point of view, tapped into a very commonly understood environmental dispute to build character. One wonders whether these sorts of portrayals influence viewers in their evaluation of pro- and anti-hunting positions.

In another event typical of the way sitcoms deal with the environment, the *Royal Family* went camping, bringing biodegradable and ozone-friendly products along with them. In this episode, the environment (i.e., the camping milieu, simulated on a soundstage) was the enemy of the family's accustomed urban comfort. The green products seemed an obvious sop to Hollywood's 1991-vintage environmentally correct ideology. This theme (what happens to an "urban" family in the sticks) has been used often to comedic effect in television programs, most notably in *Green Acres*. The *Royal Family*, as a Black family, was especially suitable for such comedy because "urban" African Americans are oftentimes stereotyped as especially unaware of nature and uncomfortable in the country.

In another confrontation between Blacks and the environmental issue, an episode of *Cosby* addressed stereotypes of young Black males. Dr. Huxtable was speaking to a class of students on this issue as a concerned member of the community. Two of the youths were joking about how they get "blamed for everything bad" that happens in society. They commented to humorous effect how they might be blamed for the "greenhouse effect" and one character said, "If whales are missing, we stole it!" Here, the joke simply appropriates topics that were in discussion at the time. Although the joke seems a stretch, the lukewarm environmental reference is fairly typical of what a viewer might have seen in the early 1990s environmental hype period: a connecting of virtually everything to the environmental issue through buzzword references.

The 1993 sample had more episodes to look at. On *Knot's Landing*, recycling was part of a public service punishment meted out to a character. Similarly, recycling appeared on *Major Dad*, when the major jokingly indicated that he planned to spend a particular day recycling. Both actions were very quick in the scheme of the show, but they do indicate how Hollywood script writers had been persuaded to include mentions of environmental themes in their shows. Offices such as the Environmental Media Association had been established to promote references to environmental issues in programs, with noticeable effect in the early 1990s. Although no measures of the effectiveness of such public relations programs exist, the programs have reportedly had less success in recent years, as Hollywood has turned its attention to other issues.

Jeopardy, as America's schoolteacher, frequently touched on environmental themes. One "answer" had to do with Chernobyl and the fact that sheep had been poisoned. On another occasion, "conservation" was an entire category of answers. Another answer concerned a spill from a Coors beer plant that killed many fish. In fact, a good many of the specific environmental references we could find in programs came from *Jeopardy* episodes. Whether this implies a "trivialization" of environmental issues is a topic for some further thought.

"Environmental correctness" sometimes became the focus of jokes in sitcoms. For instance, on *Golden Palace*, a spin-off of the popular *Golden Girls*, one character put down another by saying "you are a spotted owl in the forest of life." Or, on *Wings*, the following exchange occurred:

"Hey, if you're finished with that soda can, can I have it? I'm recycling."
"Sure, I'm all for helping the environment."
"Oh, I'm just doing it for the money to pay you back."

Sometimes environmental concerns of the past come back in old movies. For instance, in *Cannonball Run II* the characters got out of a speeding ticket by telling the officer they were carrying radioactive material from a meltdown.

On *The Commish*, a character commented "I am the social equivalent of toxic waste." On *America's Funniest Home Videos* a video trick depicted a horse with six legs. The affable host offers: "This is why you should never build a dude ranch next to a nuclear reactor."

On *Coach*, the coach visits a rainforest group to convince them that his daughter's donation is written on a bad check. He jokes: "The rainforests? Now isn't that a stupid cause, they're not even going to be around in 10 years!" The rainforests were again a focus on *Family Matters*, when a character was said to use a "rainforest tape" for relaxation, including sounds of bulldozers, chainsaws, and animals shrieking.

In a Hitchcockian twist, one of the dinosaurs on ABC's eponymously entitled show was reading a newspaper with the headline: "Environmentalists Name Top Corporate Polluters."

One wonders why producers bothered to insert such banal references to the environment in their programs. One doubts that they were motivated by deep environmental concern or influenced by paradigmatic social change. Some of this was due to publicity activities, as noted earlier. However, we conjecture that the environmental issue had become so "attractive" to Hollywood creative people in the early 1990s that they climbed onto this bandwagon of their own free will. Environmental issues, as a kind of lapel-ribbon fad, were enormously popular from about 1988 to 1992. The shows appearing in 1993 were produced during this time frame. Thus, 1993 entertainment programs probably reflect television's highest period of "attention" to environmental issues. The speed with which these references disappeared, as we see here, is comment on the cyclicality of attention to the issue.

The 1994 sample contained fewer episodes, but the ones we found were instructive. In an episode of the animated program *The Critic*, a bear is found on the set of a program. The character of the Critic asks whether the bear is stuffed, and is told: "No, the animal rights people wouldn't have allowed that. We just doped him up and propped him against the wall."

Similarly, on an episode of *Evening Shade*, a character complains that her chinchilla's hair is falling out. Burt Reynold's character provides this rejoinder: "Well, this is the 90s. They should be wearing fake fur anyway."

Such "jokes" at the expense of environmentalists and animal rights activists had been fairly common, appearing throughout our sample. By 1994, the jokes tend to predominate, whereas the earlier samples had more of a mix between serious and jocular treatments of environmental issues. By this time, television producers' adherence to environmental correctness had worn off; the producers and writers now followed a view of environmentalism as an issue whose peak had passed, leaving a set of stock "environmentalist" characters and issues that could be lampooned to good effect.

Still, 1994 revealed some respectful treatments of environmental issues. For instance, in a CBS telecast of the movie *Lethal Weapon 2*, one character is chastised by his family for eating non-"dolphin-safe" tuna. Also, in a broadcast of the *Miss USA* Pageant, one judge was presented and promoted as an "environmental philanthropist."

Finally, *Jeopardy* continued to present a few answer/questions focusing on environmental issues (A: This city in India in 1987 was the site of the world's worst industrial disaster, Q: What is Bhopal?).

In our 1995 sample, fewer episodes appeared, reflecting the continuing decrease in environmental concern. By now, even the jokes were stale. The issues discussed continued to mirror those seen in the 1994 sample, with sporadic and minor references to environmental issues in sitcoms, and so on. For instance, in the *Drew Carey Show*, one character briefly referred to the disappearance of rainforests. The program *Sea Quest* had a couple of references to environmental issues, including one joke from the captain that the crew should not shoot any sea lions because "the environmentalists wouldn't like it." On *Seinfeld*, Jerry was admonished by Kramer for littering. On an episode of *Cybil*, two characters sunbathed, clothed from head to toe. One jokes to the other: "I miss the ozone layer."

Summary: What Episodes Show. Our quantitative analysis suggests that television tends to move its characters "inward," away from nature into cities and into houses, buildings and other interiors. Frequently when nature appears it is as a test or hurdle for human endurance or achievement. Environmental issues are connected more frequently with middle-class and upper class males. Blacks and Whites partake in this environmental world in proportion equal to their TV population. Entertainers and business people play a disproportionately large role in this world.

What can we make of this? Normally, cultural indicators research tends to compare television content with real-world indicators, to see whether television distorts the real world in its presentations. For instance, rates of television violence can be compared to real-world violence to see whether one is more violent than the other (TV is far more violent, by the way).

In the case of environmental issues, however, it may not make sense to argue that television "distorts" perceptions in comparison to the real world. Rather, it may make more sense to argue that television tends to establish itself as an alternative environment. Although television shows much of the world as taking place indoors and in cities, it is wise to remember that television is also one of the reasons that so much of life takes place indoors and in cities. Television's portrayal of the world is therefore a rather interesting, if ironic, reflexive commentary on its power to cultivate images of the environment. This circularity means that it is rather difficult to compare statistics of the TV environment against the real one (although the comparison to census data on urban-rural populations is a kind of barometer of the distortion). Thus, although the television environment may play a distortive role in our perceptions of the natural world, it can also play a "replacing" role (as McKibben, 1992, suggested).

Furthermore, the environmental logic of television seems to be one in which the scene of narrative action has been created to justify the myriad lessons, purposes, goals, and outcomes of television programs. Most of these programs, designed as they are to sell products and promote consumerism, naturally ask viewers to conceive their world as a place where material goods define the environment. Echoing Barthes (1957), we think that television tends to "naturalize" this human-constructed environment to an unprecedented extent. Precisely by establishing the human-made context as not only dominant but also "hegemonic," television's conception of the environment becomes, in a sense, the dominant conception available. It is, almost by definition, a view of the environment constitutive of and highly compatible with the dominant social paradigm.

Still, as we have suggested, to gather the many separate and incidental references to the environment into a single interpretation is rather difficult. It is obvious that there is no particular "anti-environmental" conspiracy among Hollywood writers and actors. It is also rather easy to conclude that television entertainment programs are just about escapism and should not be expected to provide meaningful presentations of environmental issues. Certainly, some would argue, we should not expect our entertainment programs to provide sophisticated or diverse commentary on environmental issues, a job that should presumably be left to news.

Still, from a cultural indicators perspective, entertainment images and commentary are seen both as reflectors and shapers of predominant cultural attitudes. For the environment, this means that viewers of television are encouraged to see the environment as (in no particular order):

- a beautiful alternative to city life
- a "problem" to be solved through citizen action

- a political commitment for socially marginal types
- a source of jokes
- a source of trivia (a nostalgically fading issue that characterized a particular era)
- a test and challenge for human resourcefulness.

We argue that television's narrative "arc" between 1991 and 1995 sought to take a potentially divisive issue (what to "do" about the environment) and reconstruct it. The narrative reframing of the environmental debate, putting it on television's own terms, has been very successful. By the mid-1990s, the environmental "backlash" had found fertile ground, such that discussions of the disappearance of the dominant social paradigm now seem less compelling. Environmentalists, although firmly entrenched in government, industry, and other mainstream sectors of the civil society, had acquired a bit of the air of the lunatic. Undoubtedly, the background images and connotations of television programs about the environment have helped move along the general social trend away from environmental concern.

News

News is another "story." We found that news programs tend to deal with environmental issues more often, as one would expect. We pay less attention to news presentations in this chapter, primarily because news has been heavily examined (see chapter 2). In chapter 6, however, we examine newspaper coverage of a single story (global warming) over a 15-year period. Here we confine ourselves in a short space to some descriptive statistics on news presentations in our sample.

We "expect" environmental issues to be covered more in news, particularly their political aspects. Our sample shows that, although news programs have dealt with environmental issues more frequently, there has again been some decline in frequency of coverage in recent years. These estimates are also influenced by the sampling problem, because a "big" environmental story could well skew a sample toward the high side. Similarly, the lack of a major environmental event in our sample probably skews the sample toward the low side. None of our sample weeks included a major environmental event, such as an oil spill. Figure 4.7 shows that the percentage of news programs with environmental stories has varied widely, yet reached a low in 1995, the same year in which entertainment presentation of environmental events was at its lowest.

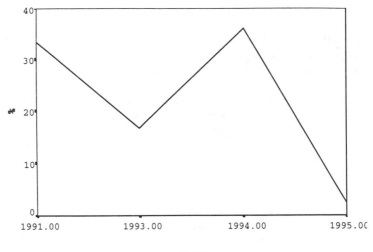

YEAR

Figure 4.7. Percentage of news programs with environmental stories

We should note that our 1995 sample contains fewer news programs due to the nature of program scheduling in the Ithaca area stations used for the 1995 sample. Nevertheless, the percentage differences are instructive. Although it is improbable that the week-long samples indicate "background" news attention to environmental issues in any given year, the entire 4-year sample gives a much better estimate of the likelihood of seeing an environmental issue in any given program: overall, about 20% of news programs have an environmental story or issue in them. This reflects the growing interest in environmental issues by news audiences (especially in the first few years of our sample), and the increasing environmental activity in government, political, and activist circles. Thus, although entertainment programs tend to push environmental attention toward the background, news is arguably drawing some attention for environmental issues.

We also coded the issues dealt with in such news stories. Figure 4.8 shows that politics, disaster, and unusual weather were the predominant environmental themes. Again, this is not surprising, given that news often points to the unusual and the conflictual. It is somewhat troubling that specific issue-based themes (recycling, energy conservation, etc.) were covered less frequently.

To show how these topics appeared and were used narratively, we compared some specific story topics to their "focus," to see what sector of the community each story focused on (business, government, science, the public, etc.). We also recorded the "tone"

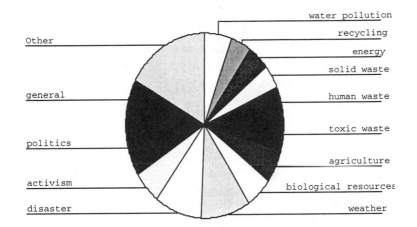

water pollution
recycling
energy
solid waste
human waste
toxic waste
agriculture
biological resources
weather
Other
general
politics
activism
disaster

Figure 4.8. Frequency of issue coverage in news programs (slices represent percentages of total)

of these stories to see whether they were "supportive," "neutral," or "critical" of the entity on which the news story focused. Table 4.4 shows a listing of selected news story topics, with their focus and tone.

First, we note that almost all of the news stories focused on either on business or the general public. Very few were focused on the government, science, or environmental activists. Although stories certainly mentioned government actions or scientific information, we found that prime-time news programmers apparently preferred to orient their environmental news toward business (new products emerging, dealing with problems posed by environmental regulations, etc.) or toward the general public (expected public reactions to problems, public opinion, etc.). In general, these presentations either tended to be neutral (i.e., objectively reporting facts) or supportive of the entity depicted in the story. For instance, a story on a company developing natural products took an overall supportive tone, implicitly supporting and promoting the idea that natural products are environmentally beneficial and that using them contributes to environmental health.

Interestingly, a majority of the critical stories in the sample focused either on the government or environmental activists, whereas all of the neutral and supportive stories focused either on business or the general public. We read this as a tendency to "depoliticize" environmental problems in news, moving them more toward the orbit of everyday business and household affairs. The

Table 4.4. Selected News Stories' Topic, Focus, and Tone.

Story Topic	"Focus"	Tone
1991—Agricultural pests	Business	Neutral
Lead lawsuits	Business	Neutral
Community cleans up a lake	Public	Supportive
Litter management	Science	Supportive
Eco-design for recycling friendly products	Business	Supportive
Energy conservation	Business	Supportive
"Natural" toothpaste	Business	Supportive
Hazardous waste "comic book characters"	Entertainment	Neutral
1993—electromagnetic fields and cancer in the home	Activists	Critical
Drilling for natural gas in culturally sensitive areas	Government	Neutral
Industry goes green	Business	Supportive
Tanker adrift	Business	Neutral
Waste issues on Cape Cod	Public	Neutral
Preservation of species on Cape Cod	Public	Supportive
Polluted beaches	Government	Critical
1994—strange weather in California	Public	Neutral
Hormone-treated cows	Business	Neutral
California business relocating due to bureaucracy and natural disasters	Business	Neutral
Heavy snows in Northeast	Public	Neutral
More unusual weather in California	Public	Neutral
Collapse of Newfoundland fish industry	Business	Neutral
Worst winter in 10 years	Public	Neutral
Business slowed by weather	Business	Neutral
Slaughterhouse conditions	Business	Critical

majority of stories, focusing as they do on business and the general public, seem to attempt to bring environmental problems, issues, and even ideology within the rubric of daily affairs. Perhaps news stories do that to highlight the system's ability to deal with environmental issues, to show that everyday people take care of environmental problems as a matter of course. On this view, environmental problems represent just the sort of challenge that can be handled by business as usual; rather than a threat to the dominant social paradigm, they are a test of the paradigm's resourcefulness (similar to the reality show's use of nature as a test). This tendency may have some benefits for environmental protection (increasing viewer perception of efficacy, perhaps). Yet, on the other hand, it seems as if such stories tend to push environmental issues toward the "lifestyle" arena. We note that this is in direct contradiction to what we observed in the entertainment programs, where nature themes were linked to other sociopolitical issues such as religion and science, and delinked from lifestyle concerns such as romance, crime, and so on.

This apparent contradiction can be partially resolved by noting that each narrative sector tends to frame the environment in a way that it is not "supposed" to. That is, television entertainment programs, geared toward narratives and lifestyle entertainment, frame the environment with other issues. Similarly, television news programs, geared toward presenting issues and information, tend to frame the environment as a lifestyle concern. In a way, this may represent the worst of both worlds for public discussion of the environment because the environment is somewhat "devalued" in each narrative "space." Without overinterpreting this admittedly conjectural explanation, we think that such a unique combination of narrative styles in the presentation of environmental issues deserves some further investigation.

Our sample did not contain any environmental disasters (although there were some stories on unusual weather patterns). We deal more with that theme in chapter 6, but we recognize that television news programs tend to treat environmental disasters differently from quotidian news presentations. There, the function of news may be to highlight the unusual and therefore attract viewers: The aim is to build viewership in a competitive environment. A frequent complaint is, in fact, that environmental news too frequently focuses on disasters and is "event-based." We are willing to stipulate at this point that our analysis has little relevance for this type of presentation. Yet our sample of stories, reflecting daily background attention to environmental issues, may have more to say about how DSP ideologies influence television content, and vice versa.

Advertising

Our final area of message system analysis concerns environmental advertising. Here, we were simply interested in the frequency with which advertisements made environmental claims as part of their selling pitch. Although the narrative aspects of advertisements are undoubtedly important components of the overall television message system, an analysis of their storylines and demographics was considered outside the scope of this volume (insofar as cultural indicators research has not normally examined advertisements).

Although some treatments of the green advertising issue have suggested that environmental ads are a fairly important sector of the market, we did not find this to be the case for television when compared to the entire body of advertisements. Studies such as those by Shrum, McCarty, and Lowrey (1995) and Banerjee, Gulas, and Iyer (1995) focus attention on environmental advertising as a growing phenomenon. Scammon and Mayer (1995) reported that 13% of all new product introductions in 1993 were for green products (a percentage that fell to 10.5% in 1994).

Although environmental advertising undoubtedly became a commercial force in the late 1980s, our sample revealed that relatively few commercials in prime-time television made environmental claims. Perhaps television was simply not the medium for the non-impulse-buying, opinion-leading consumer personified in the green buyer (Shrum et al., 1995).

We examined every advertisement in our sample to determine whether the ad made any environmental claims. For instance, gasoline products that claim to give better gas mileage were coded as *green* ads. Products that advertised their recyclability were also coded. Ads that were shot in natural backdrops were not coded as making as environmental claims (and there were a good many of these, especially car advertisements).

In our 1991 sample, approximately 1% of the advertisements we coded made environmental claims (i.e., on the average night in our sample). In 1993, this percentage increased to 1.5%. In 1994, this number dipped to 1.3% However, in our 1995 sample, environmental ads had virtually disappeared, accounting for only about 1/10 of 1% of the sample (the means are significantly different; $F = 6.6$; $p < .001$). Arguably, more than any other segment of our overall message system analysis, advertising reflected the television tendency to get off the environmental bandwagon after it had lost its trendiness.

Although some business leaders had argued that the "green consumer" would be the wave of the future, this trend never gained momentum in television advertising. Indeed, because advertising itself depends on fads and novelties to attract consumer attention, it is not surprising that advertisers and consumers turned their attention away from green advertising as a way to choose their products. Previously controversial products such as disposable diapers and gas-guzzling cars made a resurgence, as consumers forgot about environmental issues in their purchasing. Perhaps ironically, the end result of the "commodification" of environmentalism (Fink, 1990) was its own obsolescence.

DISCUSSION: DOMINANT ENVIRONMENTAL NARRATIVES

It has been widely believed throughout the 1960s, 1970s, 1980s, and 1990s that television, and mass communication in general, serve as instruments of environmental education. As seen in chapter 2, many of the tests of media effectiveness for the environment have been based on the assumption that media serve a pro-environmental educational role. However, we would argue that this fails to account for television's institutional character.

That is, television programs are designed specifically to serve as frames for advertisements. Advertisements are designed to promote the consumption of products. That these goals are fundamentally at odds with the goals of the environmental movement should be clear, particularly the sector that promotes radical environmental change and movement toward a "new environmental paradigm."

Now, undoubtedly, cases exist where television has provided important information and led many people toward thinking about problems of the environment. For instance, it is difficult to imagine thinking about issues such as Chernobyl, Three Mile Island, or the Exxon *Valdez* accident without dealing with aspects of their media coverage. In some sense, these events could not have become important contributors to environmental awareness and social action without the media coverage they received.

In another related sense, social movements stagnate without media presentation of their concerns, because all attempts to influence public opinion must eventually move through the channels of the media. Thus, if we assume that environmentalism has made any progress since the late 1960s, we must also believe that the media have played some role.

On this view, media attention to specific environmental issues is helpful for the overall ideological and attitudinal environmental cause. Yet, if one accepts that attention to specific issues is

helpful for environmentalism, it is also possible that media attention to other nonenvironmental issues might detract attention from
environmentalism, lessening its growth and importance in the civil
society. To sort out these kinds of impacts would be difficult,
requiring a kind of comparative content analysis that would prove
rather tricky. Also, such an analysis would require the assumption
that all messages tend to have equal impacts.

We are prepared to grant that media and media profession-
als have played an important, even a key role in the some of the
successes of the environmental movement. At the same time, we
feel that the incorporation of environmentalism into a media framework can dilute and even alter the messages of environmentalism.
Thus, for instance, the deeply thought and effective messages of a
book like Silent Spring can become a hysterical prophecy of doom
when translated through the popular media. The "commodification"
of environmental issues, and their media-enforced connection to
business perspectives, represent another way that media can
reframe and reorient environmental messages. More than anything,
the thoroughgoing "backgrounding" of environmental issues within
a somewhat artificially created environment of television's own
design means that new ideas about social relationships to the environment must be processed through the lens of the DSP.

For these reasons, we prefer to step back and look at how
the environment appears in the message system, at the level of the
cultural background. Although most of the images of specific environmental disasters and problems will eventually fade into memory, television's daily attention (and/or lack of attention) to the environment will, we argue, manifest a residual but lasting effect. We
think that television's conception of the environment, as revealed in
its unquestioned background images and portrayals, will affect our
own background images and conceptions of the environment—what
we call the social environment. Simply put, when we analyze television's messages at a suitably broad and deep level, we find that
conceptions and portrayals are strongly supportive of the DSP. In
this sense, we consider television programs an important propaganda arm for the dominant social conception of the environment.
Our analysis of television's dominant narrative paradigm (DNP)
suggests that its stories are highly congruent with the needs of our
social system. Thus, rather than moving individuals and our culture toward a new environmental conception, television would seem
to be retarding or even preventing such progress.

Earlier we suggested that media systems are engaged in a
narrative struggle on environmental issues. Much of the success of
the environmental movement is due to the seemingly true impression that environmental problems have become more pressing and

threatening. This image, as seen in chapter 6, is itself sometimes promoted by the media. Especially because images of disaster and doom are effective audience attractors, media message systems promote and even proactively identify problems that are potentially threatening. But far from serving an environmental surveillance function, these messages are intended solely as attractive and interesting narratives.

At this level, it might appear that television serves an environmentalist function because it attracts attention to problems and brings them into the social arena for policy solutions. Indeed, if this were the only level at which television dealt with the environment, we might well conclude that television programs serve an overall positive function for the environment.

But as issues and problems fade, viewers are left to deal with the "everyday." For television, the everyday is very closely connected to the promotion of consumerism and the selling of products. The new environmental paradigm (NEP) has not changed this at all; recent regulatory decisions in the structure of television have only strengthened television's institutional character. So, although television attracts attention to the unusual environmental event, in the background television is quietly shaping and redefining its and our conception of the natural world. As we have seen, it tends to claim environmental status for itself, and it does so without raising the question. That is, it establishes, on a daily, hourly, and minute-by-minute basis, that everyday social reality takes place within an environment whose very existence presupposes and supports the existence of the DSP.

Following this mechanism, television's environmental message has little to do with environmentalism. On prime-time TV, environmentalism eventually becomes a stale joke, while television itself has reframed and co-opted the environmental debate for its own purposes. It is "natural" that within the TV environment, environmentalists come to seem ridiculous: they can be portrayed as people who don't understand the groundrules of modern living. Yet at the same time, television can claim to be "dealing" with environmental issues. We see this as a process in which modern media systems seek to both "excite" and "soothe" people on environmental issues. Excitement works best when it leads to viewership, "soothing" works best at the ideological level. The overall goal is maintenance of the status quo.

Some implications of this for media effects research on the environment are clear. First, media research attention needs to question how attention to television programs influences viewers' beliefs and attitudes about the environment. Assuming television messages should "promote" environmental attitudes is no longer enough; it may be that they detract from or retard environmental progress. In fact, a few studies (Novic & Sandman, 1974; Ostman & Parker, 1987; Shanahan, 1993) do suggest that increased attention to television is associated with less concern for environmental issues. Until now, findings such as these could not be contexted in the knowledge that television deflects attention from environmental issues in its most important programs. Researchers have tended to interpret these results as artifacts of demographic characteristics of television viewers. Some also may argue that this deflection is due to the act of television viewing itself, which tends to detract from environmental awareness. We feel, however, particularly based on the results of our analysis in this chapter, that the messages of television may also have an important role to play in explaining these observed associations.

Furthermore, the results suggest that television, certainly the most important narrative system in our culture, tends to separate "issues" such as the environment from the "meat" of its narratives. It may be that viewer attention and narrative interest is thus focused on lifestyle at the expense of issues. Yet it is not difficult to imagine narratives that could be constructed in a way that would link environmental understanding with the audience-attracting lifestyle themes. It simply seems that television has not chosen this narrative road.

The frequency of attention to environmental issues has dropped since 1991. In our view, this decline is a symptom of an overall societal turn away from environmental issues. Major environmental issues such as acid rain and the global warming scare had propelled the environment into the cultural consciousness in the early 1990s. It appears that this attention has worn off, however, particularly as television producers and writers have apparently been less affected by the bug of environmental correctness. Moreover, the fact that television producers thought enough of the environment to include it in their scripts early on in our sample suggests that it is possible to link environmental issues with popular entertainment themes. The danger here, however, is that the dictates of entertainment require a quick succession of new and interesting topics. The environmental issue, always subject to opinion cycles, apparently lost its appeal after 1993. Television presented environmental information while it was closer to the core of popular culture and attention, but it turned attention to other issues as they became more interesting. Interestingly, the period in which McKibben criticized television for failing to deal with the environment was a time when it was focusing perhaps unprecedented attention on the issue.

When television pays attention to the environment, there are issues that it characteristically "likes." Protecting species, especially animals with a high TVQ, is an obvious way for television entertainment programs to deal with environmental issues. The popular wildlife programs, although not appearing in our sample, suggest that anthropomorphized animal stories are one way to connect environmental issues to the lifestyles that television presents. Our analysis also shows that programs focus on a relatively limited menu of environmental issues, which is not surprising because we found relatively few environmental episodes in any given week.

We do not know "why" particular issues become the focus of mass media discussion. For instance, global warming became a nationwide issue and was discussed widely on talk shows and even found its way into entertainment programs. Its currency made it fodder for the script-writing process, but also doomed it to a quick death in the media as a fad issue. It seems reasonable to assume, as with other media, that entertainment television looks at environmental issues cyclically and sporadically: Any given issue probably has a relatively short life span in the national limelight.

This does not mean that environmental issues are disappearing from television altogether. Indeed, environmental portrayals may behave according to cyclical patterns as they do in journalism. Wildlife programs have gained new life, particularly in a cable environment where channels such as Discovery have garnered profitable viewership with environmental and natural programming. Children's television has remained a haven for environmental issues as well. On the other hand, potential new sources for environmental information, such as the proposed Ecology Channel, have failed to get off the ground.

In chapter 5 we examine the impact of exposure to these messages on viewers. Using the techniques of cultivation analysis, an outgrowth of cultural indicators research, we explore relationships among exposure to television programs and environmental beliefs, attitudes, and behavior.

five

TELEVISION'S CULTIVATION OF ENVIRONMENTAL CONCERN

In this chapter,[1] we examine impacts of message systems on people's environmental conceptions. Again, the same qualifiers and disclaimers we offered in chapter 4 should apply; the measurement of understanding of narratives is a tricky and potentially misleading process. However, as we have seen, there is some observable consistency in television's presentation of the environment, so it is natural to wonder whether there is any consistency in the reception of those narratives. This chapter offers an exploratory analysis of the relationships between attention to television narratives and environmental beliefs. In turn, we produce a variety of interesting findings, some expected, others counterintuitive. But before proceeding to the data, we begin with some further theoretical offerings on media effects.

Our original interest in the relationship between television viewing and beliefs about environmental issues began in 1988. In

[1]Study 1 reported in this chapter was originally presented in Shanahan (1993). Study 2 is originally reported in Shanahan, Morgan, and Stenbejerre (1997). This chapter includes new analyses of trend data gathered from the 25-year National Opinion Research Center (NORC) trend samples. Also included is a more extensive review and discussion of results originally presented.

that year, especially in the summer, the popular press focused an enormous amount of attention on environmental issues. The almost nationwide drought and abnormal summer heat brought attention to and fear of the idea of global warming, in addition to other issues (the ozone layer, radon, medical waste on beaches, etc.), that combined to bring unprecedented attention to the environment. Capping off the spate of media attention, *Time* magazine awarded its "Man of the Year" prize to the planet Earth (which graciously accepted without a long speech). Two years later (1990), the 20th anniversary of Earth Day was celebrated, providing yet another focus for environmental news coverage and a way perhaps to attract national consciousness for environmental issues.

In addition to media presentation of environmental issues, an enormous amount of discussion centered on the role of the media in promoting environmental consciousness. It was assumed that a "positive" relationship existed between media attention to the problem and public acceptance of beliefs and attitudes consistent with a new environmental paradigm. Some journalists, esteeming themselves very important to the dawning of a new environmental era, even began to question their own standards of objectivity in favor of a journalistic advocacy for the environment (LaMay & Dennis, 1991).

Yet our view was in near diametric opposition to this position. We suspected then, and chapter 4 shows us now, that there are fads and trends in television's attention to the environment. In 1988, we supposed that the then current wave of fashionable concern would quickly attenuate. Based on this prediction, we were among the first to argue that one of the impacts of television would be a diminution or retardation of growth in environmental concern (although a few studies discussed in chapter 2 presaged this finding). As of 1997, as the wave of environmental "hysteria" has crested and receded, we have remained fairly committed to this notion, although since then we have discovered a number of important complexities and unresolved questions in the relationship between television and the environment.

In this chapter, we review our findings on television's impact on the public conception of the environment. We review our own data collected as early as 1988 (arguably the first year since the early 1970s of "high" public attention to environmental issues) and as late as 1994 (when public attention had arguably declined and was continuing to recede). We also examine relationships between TV exposure and environmental concern from 1975 to 1994 to get an idea of historical trends in the relation. Our studies use the media research method known as *cultivation* to estimate the relationships between media exposure and environmental concern.

CULTIVATION ANALYSIS

Many different methods are used to measure relations between exposure to media and environmental beliefs. As was seen in chapter 2, most studies favor an approach that examines relationships between exposure to particular environmental messages and various environmental beliefs and behaviors. As should be clear by now, however, we favor an approach that can measure relationships between message systems and broader ideological conceptions. Within cultural indicators work, the tool for doing this is called *cultivation analysis*.

Cultivation analysis is part of the overall research program that has been headed by Gerbner at the University of Pennsylvania. At base, cultivation is a theory of storytelling, which assumes that repeated exposure to a set of messages is likely to produce agreement in an audience with opinions expressed in (or attitudes consonant with) those messages. The term *cultivation* is used to indicate that the process is conceived as a cumulative one; messages and their background contexts are seen as having gradual impacts on audiences repeatedly exposed to them.

Gerbner (cited in Signorielli & Morgan, 1990) wrote:

> Cultivation is what a culture does. That is not simple causation, though culture is the basic medium in which humans live and learn. Cultivation rarely brings change except between generations and regions or among styles of life of which it is more or less a part. Cultivation is not the sole (or even frequent) determinant of specific actions, although it may tip a delicate balance, mark the mainstream of common consciousness, and signal a sea-change in the cultural environment. Strictly speaking, cultivation means the specific independent (though not isolated) contribution that a particularly consistent and compelling symbolic stream makes to the complex process of socialization and enculturation. (p. 249)

The best known use of cultivation has been to assess the impact of television viewing on societal violence, a historically frequent concern of governmental and social authorities in the United States. Generally, cultivation theory measures television exposure in individuals and attempts to associate that measurement with attitudes about any dependent variable of concern. In the case of violence, for instance, studies show that heavier television viewers are more likely to think the world is a violent place. The interpretation of cultivation researchers is that repeated exposure to the violent TV world cultivates among heavy TV viewers a perception of the world as a violent place.

The cultivation hypothesis has been tested not only for violence (Gerbner & Gross, 1976), but also for gender-role attitudes (Morgan, 1982), attitudes about aging (Gerbner, Gross, Signorielli & Morgan, 1980), racial stereotypes (Gross, 1984), intellectual skills (Morgan & Gross, 1980), socialization and peer-group affiliations (Rothschild, 1987), attitudes toward the scientific community, and a variety of other "dependent variables" (including, for instance, attitudes toward scientists and the scientific community). Most of these studies imply that television, by virtue of portraying various stereotypes and issues, actively suggests to its audiences mental constructs that are then adopted more frequently by heavy viewers.

The environmental case is somewhat different. As we have seen, the most noticeable thing about TV's attention to the environment is the extent to which the environment is ignored. There is a difference between the way television presents its environment (somewhat "passively," so to speak) and the way it presents violence (which is a visible and "active" presentation involving constant repetition). Because television actively constructs its environment as human-made and interior (i.e., indoors), it, conversely, passively constructs the natural environment as marginalized. This phenomenon is sometimes termed *symbolic annihilation* in the cultivation literature.

Cultivation research on perceptions of the elderly is another such case of cultivation in reverse. Television tends to underrepresent the elderly in its various dramatic portrayals; not surprisingly, heavy television viewers tend to have many misconceptions and stereotypes about the role of the elderly in society. Symbolic annihilation implies that viewers' interpretations about underrepresented groups will be affected. As with the elderly, so with the environment: In chapter 4 we showed that the narrative thrust of television is anti-environmental; in this chapter we argue that heavy viewers will manifest this anti-environmentalism more than light viewers. The effect might be subtle, as cultivation would predict, but it should be measurable.

Although cultivation follows social science and quantitative procedures, it is also a "critical" approach, and therefore it helps us to get at the narrative question. Critical media theory often assumes that media messages serve social control purposes and generally assumes that media institutions are effective agents of social control. That is, they presume that media have noticeable effects. Thus, to examine these "effects" quantitatively is not at odds with a critical media research project: If critical media theory is correct, then exposure to "effective" narratives should result in a tendency to absorb and adopt beliefs and behaviors consistent with those narratives. In our view, television represents a consistent and important narrative environment, which is likely to have important effects on those who most faithfully consume its messages.

The effects that can be observed are especially due to the fact that the narrative environment of television is so strongly focused on fictional entertainment. Although news programs may have registered some increase in attention to environmental issues since 1988, we observe that more than half of the U.S. television programming environment—narrative fictional programming—is devoted to pursuits that require far less attention to the environment. Thus, the bulk of television apart from news programming has remained relatively consistent in its lack of attention to the environment.

We argue that television is a key part of what Meadows (1991) termed the *informationsphere*. The informationsphere is the area of the global ecology where humans can have immediate and measurable impact by changing our informational goals and making sure that information-gathering technologies deliver environmental information with "fidelity." Television's strenuous efforts to dominate the U.S. informationsphere cannot go unheeded. Meadows argued that this informationsphere is a key contributor to the development of the anti-environmental paradigm under which we currently subsist:

> A paradigm is upheld by the constant repetition of ideas that fit within it. It is affirmed by every information exchange, in families, churches, literature, music, workplaces, shopping places, daily chats on the street. The key to paradigm stability and coherence is repetition. Therefore when people learned how to repeat information on a mass basis—to make printing presses and send messages over electronic waves—they not only created tools with the potential to improve vastly the information flows in systems, they also inadvertently invented potent techniques for paradigm affirmation and, theoretically, for paradigm change. (p. 74)

Thus, television, as a key component of the U.S. informationsphere, theoretically plays a very important role in the formation of Americans' environmental beliefs. The remainder of this chapter examines the effect of the medium of U.S. television on the general system of beliefs on environmental issues. Our studies since 1988 have focused on a single general hypothesis: Attention to U.S. television discourages the formation of pro-environmental beliefs and attitudes. Although many will disagree with this hypothesis (mirroring the widespread opposition to cultivation

research seen generally in the communication research literature),
we see in this hypothesis the simplest opportunity to assess the
contribution made by arguably the most powerful storyteller of all
time. Thus, our studies consider whether television can realistically
be considered an anti-environmental force.

We now move to two studies in which we have examined
relationships between television viewing and environmental beliefs
and concern. After we report these studies, we move to consideration of their theoretical implications.

STUDY 1

The samples for this study were taken from four undergraduate
communication classes at two large northeastern universities. One
sample was gathered in 1988 ($N = 105$), one in early 1990 ($N = 165$),
one in late 1990 ($N = 523$), and one in 1992 ($N = 230$). None of the
four samples reflect a probability design, and all are skewed in some
ways (in 1988 the sample was 61% female, in early 1990 it was 67%
female, in late 1990 it was 66.2% female, and in 1992 it was 62.1%
female). Also, compared to the general population, college students
as a group would be expected to be lighter television viewers and to
be more concerned about the environment. Despite these limita-
tions, our main concern was to explore relationships among variables rather than to make population projections about baselines.

The first wave of data collection, in Spring 1988, occurred
before the heavy barrage of environmental issues in the news during the Summer of 1988 and the Fall presidential campaign. The
second wave of data was collected in Spring 1990, after the environment had become a major news issue but before the publicity of
Earth Day in April. The third wave of data was gathered in October
1990, some 6 months after Earth Day, deep in the middle of the
Kuwaiti oil crisis (leading up the Persian Gulf War). The final wave
of data was collected in early Winter 1992, with the environment on
the backburner due to presidential politics (the environment barely
dented the public agenda, whereas Bill Clinton's personal life
received reams of coverage) although Albert Gore's volume on environmental policy was released during the sampling period, creating
a few media "events" in the process. In all years, respondents
answered nearly identical survey instruments. Although this is not
a "panel" study, having four waves allows at least for a general
analysis of trends over time.

The instrument had several parts. First, respondents were
asked about the level of importance they assigned to 18 social

issues, both environmental and nonenvironmental, ranging from reducing nuclear weapons to assuring economic growth to finding a way to stop acid rain. A five-point scale ranging from 1 (*very concerned*) to 5 (*not at all concerned*) was used for each issue. One item in the list was simply "the environment," which we refer to in this study as the general "one-item" measure of environmental concern.

Respondents then answered a battery of questions comprising a "concern inventory," loosely based on an environmental inventory created by Weigel and Weigel (1978), but updated to measure more contemporary issues. Finally, each respondent reported media use. In addition to amount of television viewing, frequency of viewing of television news and newspaper reading were also measured.[2]

From this inventory, four subscales were created, based both on conceptual decisions and exploratory factor analyses. The specific scales were:

- "Environmental Optimism: six items that asked respondents to state their agreement with statements that predicted the future environmental health of the planet (e.g., "We shouldn't be too concerned about things like acid rain and the ozone layer, because they will take care of themselves in time").[3]
- Four items addressing the relative importance of environmental issues compared to economic and technological progress (e.g., "The good things that we get from modern technology are more important than the bad things like pollution that may result").[4]
- Four items composing an index of attitudes toward specific issues that are the focus of much contemporary activism and concern (e.g., "Companies should stop using plastic for food packaging, even if it costs consumers more at the grocery store").[5]
- Three items assessing the perceived potential personal impact respondents feel they have in affecting the environmental situation (e.g., "It doesn't matter what I do, the

---

[2]Reliability analysis for the entire inventory produced a high Cronbach's alpha of .85 in 1988, .85 in early 1990, .85 in late 1990, and .83 in 1992.

[3]1988 alpha = .77, early 1990 alpha = .70, late 1990 alpha = .72, 1992 alpha = .71

[4]1988 alpha = .63, early 1990 alpha =.62, late 1990 alpha = .63, 1992 alpha = .65

[5]1988 alpha = .65, early 1990 alpha = .72, late 1990 alpha = .69, 1992 alpha = .68

environmental problem is too big for any one person to have any impact").[6]

Findings

In the first two samples, all media exposure levels remained statistically constant. Between early and late 1990, however, our surveys registered a decline in TV viewing, which we provisionally attributed to the change of sample sites from a public to a private university. Thus, the results from the first two samples are not completely comparable to the latter two samples. However, despite these differences, the relationships between media exposure and environmental beliefs were remarkably similar across the first three samples, with only the fourth sample suggesting the possibility of change.

As we might expect, baseline levels of environmental concern between increased between 1988 and 1990. Table 5.1 shows that all categories of concern demonstrated increases in environmental concern between 1988 and late 1990, particularly for con-

Table 5.1. Changes in Environmental Concern, 1988-1992.

Scale	1988	Early 1990	Late 1990	1992	F Ratio	Sig.
Overall inventory	63.71	67.38	69.68	66.93	17.46	$p < .001$
Optimism	22.27	23.25	23.58	22.78	6.71	$p < .001$
Relative importance	14.63	15.47	15.74	14.99	8.62	$p < .001$
Issue concern	12.88	14.20	15.62	14.94	37.73	$p < .001$
Personal impact	10.65	11.39	11.70	11.23	10.65	$p < .001$

Note. Scale ranges—Overall inventory: 18-90; Optimism: 6-30; Relative Importance and Issue Concern: 4-20; Personal Impact: 3-15. High values signify greater concern.

[6]1988 alpha = .41, early 1990 alpha = .40, late 1990 alpha = .51, 1992 alpha =.53. The Personal Impact measure reveals quite low internal homogeneity. Data for this measure are reported but should be interpreted with caution.

cern about specific issues and for the general inventory itself. Compared to 1988, respondents in early and late 1990 felt less optimistic about the future of the environment and ascribed greater relative importance to environmental matters. Thus, as measured by these samples and as would be hypothesized, environmental concern increased between 1988 and 1990, reflecting the general social trend toward more attention to the environment.

However, environmental concern fell between late 1990 and 1992. The overall inventory registered a nearly three-point drop, bringing the measure below where it was in the late 1990 sample. This decline is probably due to the fact that economic issues had replaced environmental ones in the minds of most Americans, per-haps especially for the college students in this last sample. Although people were still "calling themselves" environmentalists, they were objectively less concerned when measured on a variety of important environmental issues.

To what can we attribute these fluctuations in concern? Although the overall level of concern increased notably over the first three samples, these samples nevertheless showed significant negative associations between overall television exposure and environmental concern. The tests with the detailed inventory of environmental concern show that heavier viewers, as a rule, were less environmentally concerned than their lighter viewing counterparts. Correlations between media usage and the environmental attitude scales are shown in Tables 5.2 and 5.3. For the overall inventory in the 1988 and 1990 samples, a moderate, negative, and significant

Table 5.2. Partial Correlations of Television Viewing with Environmental Attitude Scales (1988, 1990, and 1992).

Index	1988 n = 105	Early 1990 n = 165	Late 1990 n = 523	1992 n = 230	All samples N = 1,023
Overall inventory	-.22*	-.18*	-.18***	-.05	-.19***
Relative importance	-.19*	-.14*	-.13**	-.05	-.14***
Specific issues	-.19*	-.16*	-.16***	-.01	-.19***
Personal impact	-.16*	-.15*	-.11**	-.07	-.14***

Controlling for age, gender, political affiliation, and political activism. *** $p < .001$; ** $p < .01$; * $p < .05$.

Table 5.3. Partial Correlations of News Viewing and Newspaper Reading with Environmental Attitude Scales (1988, 1990, and 1992).

			TV News Viewing		
Index	1988 n = 105	Early 1990 n = 165	Late 1990 n = 523	1992 n = 230	All samples N = 1,023
Overall inventory	-.06	-.12	-.12**	-.06	-.09**
Relative importance	-.02	-.10	-.10*	-.03	-.07*
Specific issues	-.11	-.09	-.04	-.14*	-.04
Personal impact	-.04	-.04	-.08*	-.05	-.06*

			Newspaper Reading		
Index	1988 n = 105	Early 1990 n = 165	Late 1990 n = 523	1992 n = 230	All samples N = 1,023
Overall inventory	-.05	.04	.00	-.03	.05
Relative importance	-.16	.00	-.19*	.06	-.02
Specific issues	-.03	.10	.02	-.11*	.09**
Personal impact	-.02	.02	.01	-.07	.02

Controlling for age, gender, political affiliation, and political activism. *** $p < .001$; ** $p < .01$; * $p < .05$.

association appears between the amount of viewing and environmental concern that stands up under controls in the first three samples. The same pattern holds for each of the inventory's subscales, also again in the first three samples.

In the case of the optimism measure, we found a relationship between heavy viewing and the tendency to believe that the future of our environment is secure. Heavy viewers were also less concerned about the specific issues that threaten the environment. In the relative importance index, the negative relationship indicates that heavy viewers tended to assign less importance to the environment than to other issues. Heavy viewers also tended to see themselves as having less personal impact on the environment (although, recall the low alpha for this measure).

Thus, most correlations with amount of television viewing were negative and significant; heavier viewers consistently expressed lower levels of environmental concern. The patterns were remarkably consistent between the three samples, despite significant overall increases in environmental concern in those years.

This tends to go against the suggestion that media attention to the environment results in greater socioenvironmental concern. That television's heavy viewers tended to be less environmentally concerned suggests the opposite: Television's messages place a kind of "brake" on the development of environmental concern, especially for heavy viewers. Because of the study's design, we cannot assess whether exposure to environmental images or information in 1988 resulted in increases in environmentalism later in 1990, even for the heavy viewers. We do address the causal issue somewhat later. Cultivation, however, assumes that fluctuation in attention to specific issues does not have as much impact on attitudes as general patterns of television content. From this perspective, it seems more plausible that the increasing socioenvironmental attention of 1988 to 1991 was generated from a variety of sources (including media other than television). This social attention, had it been operating in an environment where TV exposure did not attenuate the environmental concern of its heaviest viewers, could have resulted in even more growth in social commitment to environmental ideas.

Thus, working from these data, we hypothesized that environmental concern could have grown faster without the "retarding" influence of television. Still, we do not pretend that our data prove the argument. Our cross-sectional findings in this first study were among the first to show that increases in news attention and general media attention to environmental issues might not necessarily be having the desired impact across the board. Yet, there were paradoxical findings even in this first sample. In the final sample (1992), the negative relationships we saw with television viewing and environmental concern were not present. In fact, the partial correlation coefficients were all close to zero and nonsignificant. The relationships did not switch and become positive, but the data suggested that some years of marginally increasing concern in television programming was perhaps finally having some impact. For heavy television viewers, 3 to 4 years of increasing media attention to environmental issues seemed to be resulting in a situation where virtually everyone was as pro-environmental as everyone else.

To resolve this question somewhat, we decided to look at trend data to help clear up the picture. Fortunately, the General Social Survey (GSS) of the NORC (1994) contains data both on television viewing and environmental attitudes, from the years 1975 through 1994. This database provides, as far as we are aware, the only way to compare trends in television viewing to environmental attitudes across a significant time span. Certainly there are no truly "longitudinal" studies or data sets to allow for the same analysis (i.e., no studies follow the same individuals over time; the GSS samples new individuals each year so trends in sample averages can be followed). Our own four samples provided the ability to make some judgments about smaller trends, but the GSS data are particularly helpful in that the samples are larger (about 1,500 for each individual year in the analysis), more representative, and randomly drawn.

However, the GSS has asked only one environmental question in every sample year since 1975. That question asks respondents to determine whether they think the government is spending *too much, too little,* or *about the right amount* of money on "improving and protecting the environment" in the United States. This question has often been used as a general barometer of environmental sentiment in the U.S. population (Dunlap & Scarce, 1991). In 1990, about 70% of respondents in the GSS felt that the government was not spending enough on the environment. Yet in the 1993 GSS data, that number fell to around 60%, comparable to where it was in 1985 and 1974. Downs' (1972) argument that environmentalism behaves according to an "issue-attention cycle" seemed reasonable in view of these ups and downs.

Our analysis consists of plotting the changes in response to this question over the years, both to ascertain the general variance in response to the measure and to compare this variation across light, medium, and heavy viewership groups. Figure 5.1 shows how environmental concern, measured using the GSS item, has varied since 1975.

The graph shows that, relatively speaking, environmental concern was at a low at the earliest point in the sample (late 1970s).[7] Moving into the 1980s, levels of environmental concern began a trend toward higher concern that continued unabated until the turn of the decade (i.e., more people thought the government wasn't spending enough money). Since about 1990, in these samples, environmental concern has receded as the scale values have drifted back upward (i.e., toward the answer "government is spending too much").

This cycle reflects the Downsian phenomenon discussed earlier (see chapter 1 and 6) and shows the extent to which environmentalism, for a variety of not clearly understood social reasons, has moved up and down with time. Our depiction of the fig-

---

[7]In the figure, lower scale values are characteristic of greater support for environmentalism (i. e., lower values suggest belief that government is not spending enough on the environment).

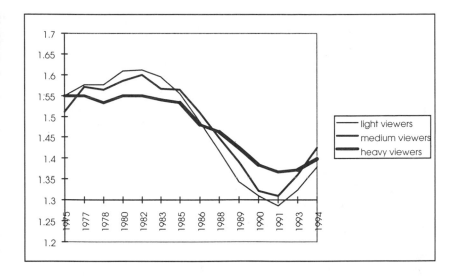

Figure 5.1. Yearly trends in response to the question "How much is the government spending on environmental health?" (4-year moving averages)
Note. Scale values are 1 (too little), 2 (about right), 3 (too much). Thus, lower scale values reflect more environmentally "concerned" positions

ure also shows the variation in the three viewership groups across the years in this trend analysis. It is clear that light, medium, and heavy viewers alike tend to move up and down in tandem, suggesting that television viewership alone does not account for variance in environmental concern (otherwise viewership groups would have moved in different directions across the trend sample).

However, it is quite noticeable that heavy viewers were slower to move toward a more environmentally-concerned position throughout the 1980s and were slower to rise back toward a less environmentally concerned position in the last few years of the sample. This observation is very consistent with the hypothesis that we advanced earlier: Television messages retarded growth in environmental concern.

This explains how we could observe negative relations between media use and environmental concern in our college samples while across the trend years environmental concern was increasing: Television messages were retarding growth caused by other factors such as personal experiences, informal communication, and so on. Also, we should note that the trends from the four college samples match closely the trends observed in the GSS samples: Environmental concern increased in the years from 1988 to 1991 and began to decrease in 1992. This gives added confidence that our college samples and the GSS samples are measuring the same phenomenon.

Essentially, Figure 5.1, taken together with results from our college samples, gives a picture of heavy viewers as more "resistant" to socioenvironmental change (heavy viewers remain closer to the temporally averaged mainstream than light or medium viewers). Thus, although the messages of television did not have the power to overcome the social and environmental changes taking place, they did retard the growth of adherence to beliefs consistent with the "new environmental paradigm." We conclude that television's narratives and narrative systems should therefore be seen as a brake on the development of "new paradigm" environmental beliefs (consistent with the theoretical arguments of earlier chapters). Indeed, the results suggest that media researchers should explore this mechanism (retardation of social change) for a variety of other sociopolitical variables as well.

Still, some researchers contend that measuring overall television exposure is not a good way to assess potential effects for the environmental issue. Wouldn't news programs have more of an impact? This is a traditional objection to cultivation research (see Potter, 1994). Yet, as pointed out in chapter 2, most of the specific media campaign and program studies have shown generally weak effects on audience attitudes. Although we feel the overall television exposure measure provides needed and overlooked information about this problem, we also measured broadcast and print news exposure to compare any possible relationships. As Table 5.3 shows, in contrast to overall television exposure, exposure to news media (electronic and print) was not positively related to environmental attitudes. This finding should surprise those who expect information consumption to promote better understanding of and adherence to environmental goals. Typically, we would assume that television news viewing would actually add to environmental concern by virtue of its increasing portrayals of these important issues. Yet our studies showed that amount of television news viewing had generally negative, weak and sometimes nonsignificant associations with environmental attitudes, especially in the first three samples. However, the final sample showed a nonsignificant but positive relations, reversing the trend of the three previous samples. This reversal was especially notable where respondents expressed opinions on specific environmental issues, many of which receive more play in the press than other, less tangible, environmental problems.

In general, however, heavier news viewers were not more environmentally concerned. Thus, it seems unlikely that news viewership would have the same "retarding" effect as overall TV exposure was shown to have. That news portrayals might have an accelerating effect also seems doubtful. Frequency of newspaper reading was also not significantly associated with environmental concern in any sample year. Again, only on specific issues did any hint of a positive relation appear, although the patterns have varied without stability across the samples and do not warrant much conclusion.

Again, however, our study does not measure effects across time, so it is possible that issue coverage may have had effects at a later time not captured by our study (in chapter 6 we investigate whether newspaper reading has retarding or accelerating effects on environmental beliefs). The instability of relationships in the 1992 sample also suggests the possibility of cumulative changes in the media-attitude relationship based on some years of continuing media hype for the environmental issue. But as seen in chapter 4, 1992 marks a decline even in the growth of sporadic media attention to environmental issues, suggesting that the weak to nonexistent relations of the 1992 sample would probably revert again to the negative within a few short years.

It may also be argued that television viewing would likely be associated with an overall lack of concern for all kinds of issues because television in general cultivates "alienation" and stifles activism. Although this may be true to some extent, we did not observe it in these data. To explore the issue, we divided the various issues that were presented to respondents into two categories: environmental and nonenvironmental. For the most part, viewing was positively associated with concern about nonenvironmental issues whereas it was negatively associated with concern about environmental issues. This suggests that television specifically cultivates nonconcern about environmental issues.

Additionally, we looked at associations with environmental concern and television in various subgroups to examine whether there were important or amplified patterns in these various groups. This technique is commonly used in cultivation analysis when demographic variables are likely to play an important role in explaining variance for the dependent variable. Figure 5.2 presents one of these analyses, using political activism as a control. Specifically, we wanted to see whether the respondent's perception of his or her own political activism was an important factor in relation to environmental concern across different levels of viewing.

The figure shows that environmental concern decreases as viewing increases, both for people who were less and more politically active. However, the decrease is steeper among politically active

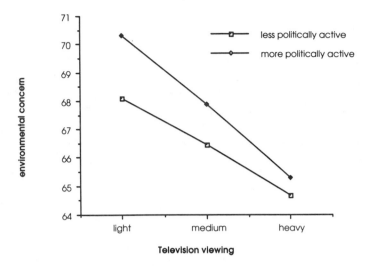

Figure 5.2. Relationship between viewing and environmental concern, by political activism

respondents, producing an overall pattern termed *mainstreaming* in the cultivation literature. The theory of mainstreaming suggests that one of the impacts of television is to produce "agreement" in groups of heavy viewers who would otherwise disagree based on other demographic characteristics. In this case, political activism differentiates high from low concern to an extent, but the difference in concern is narrowed significantly among heavy viewers. The implication is that television's consistent stream of messages is associated not only with simple changes in attitude, but also with drawing groups "closer" to the cultural mainstream that television represents. According to these data, the television mainstream is closer to the lower end of the environmental concern scale. This is also consistent with the trend data showing heavy viewers slower to change across the years.

The mainstreaming issue is key for interpreting the other patterns we have seen. Although negative relationships between television viewing and environmental concern may be attributable to "third" variables (although we normally control for the important ones), it is much more difficult to provide a compelling account for the relationships observed in mainstreaming situations, where the only likely explanation may be that television messages produce a tendency toward ideological agreement among sectors that would otherwise differ. That is, respondents who are specifically different on some demographic variables are much more similar as a function of viewing. Although "fourth" and "fifth" variables may explain such patterns, none have yet been posited that consistently explain observed mainstreaming relationships; thus, our account, which sees messages and message systems as having effects, remains compelling

Discussion

The results of this study contradicted the commonsense notion that media exposure has increased environmental concern, because increases in environmental concern were registered while negative relationships between exposure and attitude were being observed. With regard to press coverage, the extent of a relationship is even smaller, or nonexistent. One would expect positive relationships between media exposure and environmental concern if media did play a strong role in increasing environmental concern.

The data from Study 1 suggest that the overall ideological message of television is either "contradictory" to the newly emerging environmental ideology or (if the 1992 sample was indicative of a trend) perhaps only just catching up with some of the tenets of this ideology. Of course, other factors could play a role in the relationships we observe. For instance, heavy television viewers are probably simply less likely to go outside, and so they have less personal "investment" in and understanding of environmental problems. In any case, we do not argue, based on the data from Study 1, that television viewing causes lack of environmental concern (whether television "causes" anything is a difficult question to answer, insofar as it is a vital component of a complex social system). Even the trend data, although suggestive of a causal role for television messages, are not truly longitudinal, which would provide the final argument for causality. We are suggesting, however, that television is a key player in the way the culture receives and interprets messages, and messages about the environment are no exception to this rule. Thus, television's role, if not directly causal, can be seen as a systemic factor that can work against environmental improvement.

In completing Study 1 we considered how this cycle might work at the individual level. In a brief thought experiment, we began with an individual who is, as many people are "on the average," uninformed about environmental problems and not very likely to do much about them. If we imagine this person as a heavy viewer of television, our results show that he or she will be less likely to be responsive to environmental concerns and less likely to change personal behaviors for environmental reasons. Television might not have "caused" the lack of environmental concern in this imaginary subject (it was hardly "caused"; we see it more as a mental feature of 20th-century existence), but viewing may certainly have reinforced or even "reconstructed" the lack of concern.

Now if we imagine this person as a lighter viewer of television, the force of the main cultural storyteller is lessened. That yields greater chance for exposure to environmentally concerned messages in the alternative press, in interpersonal communication, and even just in communication between the individual and the environment.

Indeed, it would seem that the less we mediate our communication with the environment, the more we are likely to see it as a "real" problem. Mass media, insofar as they can provide only a simulacrum of a "real" environmental experience, are not the only or best solution. Indeed, in their current institutional framework, they seem to be a hindrance.

STUDY 2

Study 1 gave some consistent and intuitive results. However, the college samples were imperfect because they were samples of convenience. The GSS samples had the advantage of covering a longer time trend, but only one question was used. Thus, when the GSS implemented an environmental "module" in its 1993 and 1994 samples, we saw an ideal opportunity to further explore relationships between television viewing and environmental beliefs. We continued to explore the relationship between exposure to media and support for environmental issues.

Hypotheses and Rationale

The GSS environmental module included various items that allowed us to construct measures for willingness to make financial sacrifices for the environment; apprehension about specific pollution sources; feelings about the relationship between science, technology, and the environment; and level of environmental and scientific knowledge.

We tested four hypotheses that were suggested by Study 1:

Hypothesis 1: Heavy viewers are less willing to make personal sacrifices for environmental reasons.
Hypothesis 2: Heavy viewers are less concerned about the effects of pollution from typical sources such as chemicals, automobiles, nuclear power, and so on.
Hypothesis 3: Heavy viewers are more likely to believe that science and technology do not generally harm the environment.

Hypothesis 4: Heavy viewers are less knowledgeable about environmental issues.

The GSS scales we constructed (see below) generally mirrored those we used in Study 1, although more pollution-specific items were included in the GSS study.

Methods

Sample. The GSS is administered via personal interviews to a national probability sample of Americans aged 18 and older. The GSS also cooperates with international organizations to constitute the International Social Survey Program (ISSP). Each year, about 12 ISSP nations ask a specific set of questions known as a *module.*

In 1993 and 1994, an ISSP module dealt with "the environment." The module consists of 23 questions about people's attitudes regarding the natural environment. These ISSP modules represent one of the most complete and certainly recent accounts of environmental opinion in the United States (the number of completed cases in the NORC 1993 and 1994 samples was 4,598). This study uses selected questions from the module to construct scales measuring different aspects of environmentalism.

Measures. We developed five scales to represent key aspects of environmentalism. Not all questions in the module were ultimately used. Our first scale measured willingness to make financial sacrifices for the environment. Three questions asked respondents if they would pay higher prices in general, pay much higher taxes, and accept cuts in their standard of living to protect the environment. Respondents used a five-point scale to indicate degree of willingness. The items were unidimensional (dimensionality for all scales was confirmed through principal components factor analysis), and they produced a highly reliable scale (1993 and 1994 Cronbach's alpha = .85). In our summed scale, high values indicate more willingness to sacrifice for the sake of the environment. We consider such willingness a key aspect of environmentalism.

The second scale measured the tendency to see human science and technology as having a "negative" impact on the environment. Four statements are used in the construction of this scale, such as "Any change humans cause in nature—no matter how scientific—is likely to make things worse." Respondents agreed or disagreed with the statements of this scale along a five-point continuum, with agreement representing, for us, an environmentally "concerned" position. These items are unidimensional and the scale has a reliability of .61 (.64 in 1994). High scores on this scale reflect the belief that science and technology are "bad" for the environment.

The next two scales dealt with the perception of threats from different kinds of pollution. The ISSP module asked respondents whether they think pollution caused by various sources is "dangerous to the environment." Responses were made from a five-point scale, ranging from 1 (*extremely dangerous*) to 5 (*not at all dangerous*). The question was asked for nuclear power, automobile pollution, industrial air pollution, agricultural chemicals, water pollution, and the greenhouse effect. These six questions empirically tap a single dimension of perceptions of "general" environmental threat. The items were unidimensional with a high reliability of .80 (.82 in 1994). Higher values reflect a higher perception of pollution as dangerous.

Respondents were also asked about the extent to which these same pollution sources posed a threat to them and to their families. These six items also form a single factor, reflecting how much individuals think pollution is a "personal" factor in their lives. Reliability for this scale is also high at .85 in both 1993 and 1994. Again, higher values reflect a greater perception of danger.

The next scale deals with environmental "knowledge" and is measured simply by tallying "correct" answers to a series of environmental test questions posed by the ISSP module. There are seven test questions, such as "The greenhouse effect is caused by a hole in the Earth's atmosphere." For each item, the "correct" response was self-evident. Respondents answered using a four-point scale ranging from 1 (*definitely true*), 2 (*probably true*), 3 (*probably not true*), to 4 (*definitely not true*). Correct answers were coded "1" while incorrect answers and "don't knows" were coded "0." Respondents who qualified their answers with "probably" were grouped with those who gave definite answers. Scores were then summed to create a scale ranging from 0 to 7, with 7 as the most knowledgeable score. Reliability for the knowledge scales was low (less than .40), but because it is a simple account of respondents' ability to correctly respond, their lower reliability does not impede analysis. Still, we interpret it cautiously. Descriptive information for all scales is presented in Table 5.4.

The NORC measure of television exposure asks viewers to report "about how many hours" of television they watch per day. Mean viewing in the 1993 sample was 2.9 hours per day (which is very close to other nationally reported averages). In the 1994 sample, mean viewing was 2.82 hours. For many analyses in this study, we trichotomized television viewing into categories of light, medium, and heavy viewing. These trichotomizations are used to show descriptive patterns that might not be evident in statistics

Table 5.4. Descriptive Information for Dependent Variable Scales.

	Year	Mean	Std Dev	Minimum	Maximum	N
Willingness to sacrifice	1993	9.11	3.03	3.00	15.00	1438
	1994	8.72	3.03	3.00	15.00	1298
Perception of threat from science and technology	1993	11.76	2.78	4.00	20.00	1354
	1994	11.55	2.88	4.00	20.00	1209
Perception of danger to the environment from pollution	1993	21.91	3.99	11.00	30.00	1232
	1994	21.46	4.06	8.00	30.00	1048
Perception of danger from pollution to self and family	1993	20.82	4.43	6.00	30.00	1224
	1994	20.58	4.38	7.00	30.00	1045
Environmental knowledge	1993	4.39	1.42	0.00	7.00	1468
	1994	4.31	1.44	0.00	7.00	1332

Note. All scales were constructed as simple summed indices. The environmental knowledge scales were constructed on the basis of seven dichotomously (re)coded variables. All other scales used variables coded on a five-point continuum.

using continuous data. When calculating statistics such as correlations, we use the continuous data. In our sample, light viewers watched 1 hour or less per day, medium viewers 2 to 3 hours per day, and heavy viewers four or more hours per day. These are self-reported amounts. This trichotomization does not divide the sample into perfect thirds, but it comes as close as the frequency distribution permits. Demographic measures used in this study are age, gender, education (years completed), SES (using NORC's socioeconomic index [SEI]), political self-identification (liberal/moderate/conservative), and size of population of hometown.

Results

To begin, we examine whether environmentalism is higher or lower among heavy viewers of television for the sample as a whole, replicating the analysis of Study 1. As Table 5.5 shows, some relationships exist, although not all of them are in the direction predicted by our hypotheses.

The results show that heavy viewers are less likely to be willing to sacrifice financially for environmental reasons. However, multiple partial controls reduce the association to zero. Heavy viewers are also more likely to think that science and technology are bad for the environment. This relationship is stronger, but it runs counter to the hypothesis that television cultivates environmental apathy in support of technoconsumerist culture. This association remains significant under multiple control, both in 1993 and in 1994.

Essentially no bivariate relationship appears between television viewing and perception of specific threats to the environment such as industrial air pollution or the greenhouse effect. Although heavy viewers may fear the negative environmental impacts of technology or science, they do not fear the specific sources of pollution as much, or at all. Neither are heavy viewers significantly more fearful that pollution will affect themselves or their family.[8] Finally, as predicted, heavy viewers are less knowledgeable about environmental issues, both in 1993 and in 1994. However, only the 1993 association remains significant under multiple control.

Thus, the overall findings are mixed with respect to the hypotheses we advanced, yet the bivariate relationships only tell part of the story. Simple associations can obscure meaningful subgroup relationships and suggest relationships when there are in

---

[8]We can also find an explanation of these phenomena in the the literature on risk communication, which suggests that media affect societal-level risk judgments but not personal-level judgments.

Table 5.5. Relationships Between Television Exposure and Dependent Variables.

Dependent variable	Light		Medium		Heavy		Corr. (1)	
	1993	1994	1993	1994	1993	1994	1993	1994
Willingness to sacrifice	9.78	8.97	8.91	8.98	8.86	8.25	-.07**	-.06
							-.02	-.01
Perception of threat from science/technology	11.24	11.31	11.52	11.40	12.65	12.47	.23***	.21***
							.13***	.13***
Perception of danger to the environment from pollution	22.12	21.34	21.56	21.60	22.37	21.51	.04	.05
							.04	.07
Perception of danger from pollution to self and family	20.84	20.59	20.55	20.59	21.30	20.74	.05	.06
							.03	.06
Environmental knowledge	4.76	4.55	4.42	4.32	4.01	4.08	-.18***	-.11***
							.07*	.00

$p < .05$ **; $p < .01$ ***; $p < .001$
(1) The first row of correlations reported are simple Pearson's rs. The second row are partial correlations, controlling for all demographic variables in study.

fact none. For each scale, then, we undertook an analysis to show associations between environmentalism and television viewing in various important subgroups.[9]

The relationships between viewing and environmental sacrifice differ somewhat in subgroups (see Table 5.6). Females are more willing to sacrifice than men, but less so as heavy viewers, particularly in 1993. The relationship is especially strong for self-identified liberals in both sample years. Also, urban dwellers are more likely to support sacrifice for the environment, a finding commonly noted in environmental research (Lewis, 1992). But urban dwellers do not demonstrate this support as strongly if they are heavy viewers, and they substantially resemble rural respondents in attitude. High education respondents display more of a relationship with television viewing, as do high SES and older respondents.

In most of these cases, one subgroup is more responsible for the observed overall association between attitude about sacrifice and television exposure. Usually the more environmentally "friendly" group—in this case, those more willing to sacrifice—find themselves less willing to sacrifice as heavy viewers. This is the mainstreaming pattern already discussed. Figure 5.3 shows the relationship in graphic terms for political subgroups, depicting the narrowing of the range of attitude among heavy viewers.

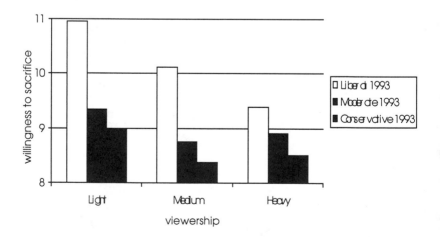

Figure 5.3. Mainstreaming of attitudes toward environmental sacrifice, in political subgroups
Note. Higher scale values signify greater willingness to sacrifice

---

[9]The knowledge scale was not included in this analysis.

Table 5.6. Relationships Between Television Exposure and Willingness to Sacrifice, in Demographic Subgroups.

	Light		Medium		Heavy		Correlation	
	1993	1994	1993	1994	1993	1994	1993	1994
Overall	9.78	8.97	8.91	8.98	8.86	8.25	-.07**	-.06
Male	9.58	8.40	8.97	9.10	9.13	8.17	-.02	-.06
Female	9.93	9.44	8.86	8.88	8.70	8.30	-.11**	-.06
Liberal	10.95	10.15	10.11	10.04	9.40	8.65	-.23***	-.19**
Moderate	9.35	8.66	8.74	8.44	8.90	8.00	-.02	-.05
Conservative	8.99	8.43	8.38	8.65	8.51	8.27	.01	.04
Rural	9.30	8.74	8.83	8.71	9.15	8.33	.01	-.04
Urban	10.25	9.28	8.99	9.22	8.56	8.20	-.15***	-.09
Low education	8.85	8.03	8.59	8.44	8.79	8.12	-.01	.03
High education	10.21	9.54	9.18	9.43	9.00	8.49	-.08*	-.09*
Low SEI	9.36	8.71	8.58	8.55	8.87	8.03	-.01	-.04
High SEI	10.06	9.16	9.18	9.42	9.06	8.56	-.09*	-.04
Younger	9.76	9.07	9.06	9.06	9.23	8.67	-.04	.00
Older	9.80	8.87	8.73	8.89	8.56	7.96	-.09*	-.10*

*$p < .05$; ** $p < .01$; *** $p < .001$

The relationship between viewing and fear of science/technology is strong and consistent in all subgroups (the data are presented in Table 5.7). Mainstreaming patterns are not evident. If television discourages environmentalism, it clearly does not do so by convincing people ideologically of the "health" or "safety" of a technoscientific culture. Either heavy viewers hold environmentally paradoxical positions (which is not impossible) or something else is happening.

As we look more closely at relationships between viewing and concern about specific pollution generating technologies, only a few subgroups show relationships; however, these relationships are in the positive direction, showing that, in a few cases, heavy viewers are more fearful (for brevity, we do not present these data in tabular form). For both pollution indices, the conservative, male, rural, and low-education heavy viewers are more concerned than their light viewing counterparts. These are subgroups that tend to be less concerned overall, offering some indication that television mainstreams viewers toward a slightly higher level of environmental "worry." Again, this finding is counter to our hypothesis, although still consistent with the view that television tends to homogenize the views of otherwise distinct groups.

Some of the cross-year comparisons show a weakening association in 1994 evident both in the lower correlation coefficients and in the comparisons for light, medium, and heavy viewers. In fact, only the relationship between viewing and apprehension about science and technology remains as strong in both years. It may be that the 1994 sample, taken during a period of lesser media attention toward the environment compared to the early 90s, shows the tendency for these relationships to become less severe as media attention on environmental issues decreases. However, this 1-year change is not something cultivation would predict. These differences may also reflect random fluctuations and sampling error (these differences are well within the scope of what statistical theory would predict; see Morgan & Shanahan, 1996).

These findings have some important political connections as well, involving whether policies should be implemented to control environmental problems. Two NORC questions allow us to address this issue. The first question states,

If you had to choose, which one of the following would be closest to your views? Government should let ordinary people decide for themselves how to protect the environment, even if it means they don't always do the right thing, or government should pass laws to make ordinary people protect the environment, even if it interferes with people's right to make their own decisions.

Table 5.7. Relationships Between Television Viewing and Conceptions of the Impact of Science and Technology on the Environment.

Viewership	Light		Medium		Heavy		Correlation	
	1993	1994	1993	1994	1993	1994	1993	1994
Overall	11.24	11.31	11.52	11.40	12.65	12.47	.23***	.21***
Male	10.58	11.13	11.34	10.99	12.52	12.14	.26***	.20***
Female	11.71	11.45	11.68	11.72	12.73	12.69	.20***	.21***
Liberal	11.58	11.06	11.28	11.51	12.45	11.90	.15**	.11
Moderate	11.02	11.33	11.98	11.55	12.93	12.43	.26***	.23***
Conservative	10.98	11.37	11.17	11.14	12.35	12.89	.25***	.24***
Rural	11.26	11.40	11.70	11.38	12.57	12.36	.23***	.18***
Urban	11.22	11.18	11.34	11.41	13.74	12.06	.23***	.23***
Low education	12.30	12.48	12.20	11.82	13.04	12.86	.18***	.16***
High education	10.74	10.62	10.97	11.05	11.83	11.84	.18***	.18***
Low SEI	12.12	12.75	12.07	11.62	12.84	12.81	.17***	.14**
High SEI	10.73	10.4-	10.88	11.25	12.10	11.75	.21***	.20***
Younger	11.24	11.41	11.47	11.50	12.77	12.40	.25***	.16**
Older	11.24	11.16	11.56	11.28	12.54	12.52	.21**	.26**

Note. Higher scale values reflect belief that science and technology are "bad" for the environment.

A similar question asks whether government should impose on business in the same way.

Respondents are surprisingly willing to have government make these choices (especially because most NORC data and other surveys show that we have little "confidence" in government). For instance, 79% think that government should make laws, leaving only 21% who think that the people should decide. In the case of business, only 9% think that businesses should be left free to decide. Clearly, there has been a certain "demonization" of the free market in the context of environmental issues. The NORC respondents demonstrate substantial fear of "normal" mechanisms of decision making in a supposedly free, pluralistic, and open-market society. However, those who do endorse the free and competitive approach are an interesting group as far as our hypothesis is concerned.

In the case of the government versus the people, heavier viewers are more likely to endorse individual solutions ($r =. 10$, $p < .01$). In the case of the government versus business, heavy viewers are slightly more likely to favor business rights, although variance is restricted by the fact that almost everyone feels the government should decide ($r = .06$, $p < .05$). This is the clearest evidence that television might "work" on environmentalism at the politico-ideological level, although these two relationships by no means prove the case. These data are consistent with the idea that ideological messages against "collective" environmental defense mechanisms (an important aspect of environmentalism as currently practiced) are encoded in television programs. If we examine only those who support nongovernmental approaches we find that these "libertarians" are heavier viewers, are more conservative, perceive less danger from pollution sources (both to the environment and to themselves), are less willing to make sacrifices, and are less knowledgeable (both scientifically and environmentally). Thus, at least for a significant minority portion of this sample, heavy viewing may work on environmentalism in exactly the ways specified by our hypothesis, namely to decrease or retard support for environmental protection.

Discussion

Clearly, the data did not fully support all of our hypotheses. Taken together with the first study, however, an intriguing picture of television's relationship with the environment emerges.

First let us quickly review the findings. If willingness to make environmental sacrifices is a feature of environmentalism, then heavy viewers are less environmentally concerned, at least in some subgroups. (Indeed this may be the most important dimension of environmentalism "retarded" by the messages of television.) On the other hand, if "distrust" of science and technology represents an aspect of modern environmentalism, then heavy viewers are more environmentally concerned. About specific pollution issues, heavy viewers are generally neither more nor less concerned (with the partial exception of nuclear and automobile issues). Finally, if environmental knowledge is higher among environmentalists, then heavy viewers are less environmentally aware, although multiple controls wipe out this association for the sample as a whole in 1994.

Without overstating the strength of support for our hypotheses, we can make some interesting conjectures about what these data suggest. Paradoxically, some of the patterns we observed suggest that television mainstreams heavy viewers toward a more environmentally concerned or perhaps even "fearful" position. Contrary to what cultivation would predict, television viewing may produce greater environmental concern through an "alarmist" mechanism. According to this view, sporadic but very alarming coverage could be producing incremental increases in environmental worry (which would also explain why the associations in our 1992 sample from Study 1 were unstable). This view would correspond to those of some social critics who see the media as feeding the fires of ignorance more than anything else. Also, it would indicate that cultivation's message system approach might not be the best method for discerning such program-specific effects because cultivation examines message systems as opposed to programs.

However, alarmist increases in environmentalism among heavy viewers do not apparently extend to behavioral intentions, and it may be possible, as Wiebe (1973) suggested, that alarmist attention to environmental information actually numbs audiences against any desire to participate in solving the problem. Moreover, heavy viewers are less knowledgeable about environmental issues. Thus, if heavy viewers are forming some environmental opinions based on television messages and are hoping to base action decisions on these opinions, realizing that these opinions are not deriving force from greater knowledge derived from media exposure is important. Although the environmental "agenda" may be determined by media coverage, the extent of correct environmental knowledge is not.

Our hypothesis is that television has portrayed environmentalism using narratives emphasizing the dangers of science and technology to the natural world without indicting particular technologies or modalities (except for nuclear power). In this way, television entertainment may coopt the excitement of possible environmental danger without producing any increase in "real" behavioral or deeper attitudinal commitment. Again, notions such as Wiebe's (1973) "well-informed futility" may be useful in understanding our findings.

A summative, theoretically coherent, view is that television messages may specifically but sporadically cultivate environmental fear because television in general uses fear, doomsaying, and sensationalism to generate attention. Environmental apprehension could then be considered a special case of TV-generated fear, already well-known from the cultivation literature. Especially interesting is the possibility that heavy viewers react to environmental problems with a "narcotized" fear (Lazarsfeld & Merton, 1971). That is, science and technology, conceived as strange and powerful agents of social management, may be seen as out of the control of the individual. This would also explain why the observed associations decreased in the 1994 sample, because these data were measured at a time further away from the early 1990s peak in environmental attention.

However, if the associations decreased in 1994 due to distance from environmental alarmism or hysteria, it suggests that specific but sporadic environmental portrayals are as important to environmental cultivation as the "background" consumerism and protechnology viewpoint we originally hypothesized. Clearly, data from longer trend intervals, as well as longitudinal data, are needed to answer these questions.

This interpretation is somewhat different than the straight "ideological" interpretation we reached after Study 1. We assumed that heavy viewers would manifest a position of direct support for tenets of the dominant social paradigm, including the notions that scientific and technological progress are helpful for the environment and humanity in general. However, reinterpreting the cultivation of environmental fear within the general cultivation literature on fear (of violence, of science, of virtually anything, really), we began to imagine that environmental fear might serve a "useful" narrative purpose. The creation of a populace well-versed in environmental dangers but ignorant of environmental realities presents an excellent opportunity for (a) the presentation of the idea that "larger forces" should handle environmental problems and (b) that environmental problems are too large too control through individual decisions. In this way, the individual consumer might well feel that purchasing and consumption habits need not change, as corporate and political forces haggle about environmental destiny. This interpretation obviously needs further support. What seems clear, however, is that television narratives have adapted somewhat to the mainstream notion that "green" is "good."

Another interpretation is that heavy viewers' "concern" about science and technology seen in these data may simply be an artifact of the already researched phenomenon of distrust of the scientist among heavy viewers. Gerbner et al. (1981) found that science and the scientific community are distrusted more among heavy viewers due to specific problems with the presentation of science on TV. They found that the "dubious imagery" of science on television, usually associated with violence and portrayals of strange alien futures, contributes heavily to the distrust of science.

Our experience with Studies 1 and 2 suggests that cultivation analysis cannot provide all the answers we were looking for (indeed, no method provides all answers). In particular, Study 2 shows that more complex narratives may be at work than a straight ideological interpretation would suggest. In chapter 7, we return to some of the questions raised by this analysis. Overall, however, we feel that our analysis strongly suggests that television may retard the speed with which social change occurs for environmental issues. This "retardation" may be due to television's meta-narrative about the environment, the residual story that is left over when all individual stories have been told.

But within that meta-narrative, as we have argued earlier, many individual stories weave in and out of each other to contribute to the whole. In the next chapter, we look at one of these stories. Because cultivation and cultural indicators are not well-suited to looking at particular narratives, we return to an interpretive analysis. To deal with the issue of environmental fear specifically, we turned our attention to how the media dealt with a single fearful issue, that of global climate change.

six

ISSUE CYCLES
AND GLOBAL
CLIMATE CHANGE*

In this chapter, we turn our attention from fictional narratives to stories of environmental "truth." Although most studies of the mediated environment have focused their attention on nonfictional narratives such as news or informational campaigns (see Chapter 2), our approach attempts to link a perspective on news narrative to our results from the entertainment/fiction sphere. We do this primarily because we see news messages as another linked component of the overall media message system. To gain a more complete understanding of the environmental impacts of news, we believe it is crucial to understand that news messages are not necessarily separate and distinct from entertainment or fictional narratives. News messages are constructed and disseminated under essentially the same institutional strictures and constraints as are fictional messages. The messages must attract attention and entertain in virtually the same manner as fictional narratives; certainly their effectiveness is measured by similar criteria. Still, news as a genre allows for a more detailed treatment of environmental issues than

*This chapter is based on a paper originally presented to the Conference on Communication and the Environment, in Chattanooga, Tennessee (March, 1995).

what we have seen in fictional mass media narratives, and there is no gainsaying that news appropriates dramatic conventions much different from those one would expect to see in fictional narratives.

A common assumption is that news messages "promote" environmental concern (at least in an agenda-setting sense); this assumption is in 180-degree opposition to the conception that we have brought to our analysis of fictional messages. If we accept this "traditional" notion of news message effectiveness, then different components of the media institution are at odds with each other as far as environmental messages are concerned. That is, although entertainment messages tend to discourage or retard environmental concern, news messages might spur or promote such concern. Depending on the "power" of news messages relative to entertainment messages, our cultivation findings might well be wiped out when news message effectiveness is taken into account.

This paradox is erased, however, if we do not begin with the assumption that news messages promote environmental concern. Although news messages may well bring about attention to and "awareness" of environmental issues, such attention may not automatically bring about environmental "concern." It is possible, for instance, that news audiences "use" issues such as the environment to provide entertainment or distraction in much the same way that they use fictional messages. If this is the case, a steady diet of environmental catastrophes and impending global disasters could serve an audience-attraction function as well as any other stream of sensational and titillating disasters. Because fear plays a special role in attracting audience attention, we turn our attention to how fearful issues are portrayed.

We have already seen in the previous chapter that not much relationship, in cross-sectional samples, existed between exposure to television news and environmental concern. On the whole, it looks as if exposure to TV news messages has little impact on individuals' environmental conceptions (and note that our finding is not new; it mirrors, generally, the findings seen in chapter 2). Thus, it is doubtful whether television news attention to the environment can be tied, in a wider sense, to increases or decreases in environmental paradigm change.

But what effects do newspaper messages have? Many studies have revealed that newspaper content tends to have different effects than messages from television. For instance, political studies show that those who get their information from newspapers tend to be more informed, more participatory, and more likely to make decisions based on issues rather than content. If the same phenomenon held true for news consumption of information about environmental issues, we might well expect to see positive relationships between exposure to newspaper content and environmental concern. Because newspapers have unquestionably given more attention to environmental issues since 1970, such a positive relationship would also explain, at least partially, the rise in public attention to environmental issues since that time. Thus, understanding the content and effectiveness of print messages when we are looking at the role played by media institutions in environmental concern is equally important.

To understand the role of print messages, we examined a particular issue—global warming or global climate change—and the coverage it received during a period of increasing public attention to environmental concern. We chose global warming because at certain points since the 1970s it has received a great deal of news coverage, yet at other times it is rarely mentioned. The issue has been subject to radical swings both in public and news attention, which makes it a special kind of issue catalyzing special kinds of questions, for example, how can public opinion (or its simulacrum in the media) have gone from a period of worrying about global warming as a possible world annihilator to a period when it hardly paid any attention at all within the span of a few short years? In this chapter, we use a narrative perspective and a trend analysis to put public attention to the issue in perspective. We see that, taken together, an understanding of news coverage of environmental issues and fictional attention to such issues reveals some interesting narrative dynamics. The chapter concludes with an analysis of the role of public attention to newspaper coverage, in general, on the environmental issue.

ISSUE CYCLES

Recent polls on the environment have indicated that it is difficult to sustain public environmental concern at uniformly high levels. Awareness of environmental issues is challenged by other issues (especially economic ones) on a regular basis (Moore, 1995), and public "tolerance" for discussion of specific environmental problems often appears to be relatively light. This observation seems particularly true in the case of attention to and concern about global warming. The situation may be partly explained by the well-known "issue-attention cycle" hypothesis of Downs (1972), who posited that environmental issues are naturally susceptible to "ups" and "downs" of public attention (see discussion in chapter 1). According to Downs' analysis, environmental issues pass through the following phases: a *preproblem* stage leads to a period of *alarmed discov-*

ery associated with specific environmental problems or hazards. This leads to *euphoric enthusiasm* being mustered to combat the problem. Then the public realizes the cost of making significant progress, and a decline of intense public interest follows. This decline leads to a post-problem phase, where attention toward the issue settles down, although at a level higher than that at which the cycle was initiated and subject to what Downs called "spasmodic recurrences of interest" (pp. 39-40).

How correct has Downs' hypothesis been? Some theorists claim outright that Downs' hypothesis does not work. Dunlap (1995) is perhaps the most well-known advocate of a view of environmental public opinion support as stable or increasing (i.e., as noncyclical). Arguing from data such as the NORC GSS, Dunlap claimed that environmentalism has avoided the cyclical decline that Downs predicted. If public opinion measures can be accepted as good indicators of general social attention to environmental issues, Dunlap provided excellent support for the thesis that Downs' hypothesis does not explain environmental issues. This support is also confirmed in other analyses of environmental public opinion (see Gillroy & Shapiro, 1986).

Seen from a different perspective, however, cycles do emerge, especially in media coverage patterns. As was seen in chapters 4 and 5, media cycles of attention on environmental issues are easily observable. Apart from natural cyclicality in human attention spans, an array of factors, some of which are discussed here, influence how media attend to issues, how they construct these issues as important or worthy of notice, and how they, in turn, can either reinforce or dampen continued coverage. In this chapter, our particular focus is on how *The New York Times* and *The Washington Post* constructed stories about global climate change and how this construction encouraged cyclical coverage from 1980 to 1994. In this chapter, we move from television data to print media data, although we think that there are important similarities between print and broadcast news coverage that warrant their side-by-side consideration.

(De)constructing Issue Cycles

In the wake of the massive amount of attention paid to the environment after the inaugural Earth Day in 1970, Downs posed the question, "How long will the American public sustain high-intensity interest in ecological matters?" (pp. 38-39). He found his answer in the issue-attention cycle. According to Downs, environmental issues are cyclical for three reasons: First, problems related to the issue are experienced unequally; not enough people suffer directly from the problems to maintain attention to the issue. Second, such problems are generated by social arrangements providing significant benefits to a majority or a powerful minority of the population. Finally, the problems themselves have no intrinsically exciting qualities, or they fade with time.

Downs' argument seems to be that these qualities inhere "naturally" in issues such as the environment.[1] For Downs, the problem of cyclical public attention and awareness is potentially insoluble because environmental issues intrinsically possess qualities that cause the public eventually to turn its attention to other more "interesting" or pressing problems. We argue that social and narrative factors distinct from the environmental issue itself influence the attention cycle. Although Downs certainly has a social perspective on the environmental issue (especially in his analysis of the structural role that media play in the dynamics of the cycle), the implication is that these social considerations are "facts" that will inalterably and immutably contextualize the development of public awareness of environmental issues. Insofar as these arrangements are social, however, significant questions of individual perception and social construction remain unanswered. In our view, it is too restricting to assume that the three reasons just cited are unchanging characteristics of the environmental issue. That is, they may be characteristics of the issue as we currently experience it, but such experience is due partly to social factors, including how mass media construct the issue.

If the issue is preeminently social, communication questions come to the fore. Communication theory would suggest, for instance, that environmental problems may be "experienced" unequally by minorities and majorities due to portrayals of the problem that do not adequately address the needs of all potential receivers of information. Structural inequity in media portrayals could be equally, or at least partly, responsible. For instance, mass media portrayals of environmental information are known to be "effective" mostly at the upper rungs of the socioeconomic ladder, with underprivileged classes receiving—or choosing to receive, remember, and utilize—relatively little information (see Bailey, 1970b, for a discussion of the knowledge gap hypothesis in relation to environmental issues; also see Griffin, 1990).

---

[1]For Downs, environmentalism is the "issue" and pollution the "problem." In our analysis, we apply the term *issue* more freely yet still limit it to environmental topics that are distinctively ongoing in nature, such as pollution. Lacking inherent beginnings, middles, and endings, issues are woven into stories that are socially constructed.

Similarly, social arrangements that influence issue-attention cycles need not be accepted as given. The information structures that help generate these inequalities can also be criticized, with suggestions made for reform. An institutional perspective on media, as we have seen, shows that communication media in the United States exist to serve purposes not in themselves environmentally sound, including the promotion of consumerism and materialism—both components of the DSP—often used to characterize the attitude state "opposite" environmentalism (e.g., Dunlap & Van Liere, 1984). Thus, although reasons exist for media to turn attention away from environmental concerns, there are also reasons for media to "use" or exploit such concerns for institutional or business purposes.

Finally, the claim that an issue must be exciting, dramatic, or sensational in order to gain public interest is, itself, a function of media systems geared toward promoting this quality. Ratings, advertising sales, and institutional competitiveness contribute to this end in large measure. Characteristically, media portrayals seek not only to cover exciting issues but also to actively construct issues as exciting. We argue there is less pregiven "excitement" inherent in an issue than Downs assumed; it is a matter of social, institutional, and communicational choice to discuss issues in that or any other way.

Recent work on the sociology of science and the construction of social issues in media has begun to point the way toward a theory of social issues that can account for their cyclical nature, as well as their connection to media constructions. Some of this work has a direct bearing on Downs' hypothesis, especially the "linearity" of his cycle. Referring to Downs' model as a "natural history" approach to the evolution of social problems, Hilgartner and Bosk (1988) argued that problems can exist "simultaneously in many stages of development." Moreover, a linear approach ignores the interactions between coexisting problems that help to define the problem as meaningful (pp. 54-55). Their alternative framework examines how social problems are articulated and propagated in public arenas, such as the media. A problem's life cycle has less to do with a measure of public opinion than with its construction in public forums. Hansen (1991) supported a similar approach in his study on media and the social construction of the environment, preferring a framework that focuses on the social problem (i.e., the environment) instead of the media coverage. He argued that media coverage is only one factor in the problem's construction and, thus, will never give a full explanation of why issues fade in and out of importance.

Most studies typically see media as an independent variable for the dependent variable of environmental public opinion, but we argue that media coverage is also "symptomatic" of social attention to environmental issues. That is, we see media portrayals and attention to environmental issues as entwined in mutually reinforcing feedback loops, where media attention to environmental issues can reinforce public concern, which can in turn encourage more media attention. Although media play an important role in the construction of attention to environmental issues, at other times the loop may have a damping effect, as low public concern produces lesser media attention, and so forth. Although this observation drastically understates the complexity of the public opinion and real-world systems that increase attention toward environmental issues, it points out that media coverage, itself, can be seen as an important "barometer" of such attention.

Aspects of our approach find their heritage in the literature on agenda setting, which examines the relationship between media attention to an issue and public opinion toward that issue (among recent reviews are Rogers & Dearing, 1988, and Protess & McCombs, 1991). Although fewer in number, some agenda-setting studies also examine how media set the agenda among themselves, thereby creating a "reinforcement" effect. Of particular interest is Trumbo's (1994) analysis of intermedia agenda-setting relationships in media coverage of global warming from 1985 to 1992. Using samples from national newspapers, national news magazines, national television networks, and the science index, Trumbo examined the similarity in the content and amount of coverage allotted to global climate change within and across media. He also checked the stability of the relationships over the 7-year period. Overall, he found a strong intermedia agenda-setting relationship. He found that during the early phase of interest in global climate change, intermedia agenda-setting relationships were most pronounced, suggesting reinforcement of the topic's salience among media. Trumbo's results strongly confirm our approach to media institutions as comprising an interlocked message system.[2] Mazur and Lee (1993) also examined the reinforcement effect in terms of how several approximately concurrent environmental news stories set the national agenda of news organizations, politicians, and the public in the late 1980s. Their study indicates that the news stories fed on one another and promoted common linkages and themes, which encouraged more media attention.

Ungar (1992) offered another related, although distinct, explanation of global climate change and the cyclical nature of attention to it by putting particular emphasis on the real-world

---

[2]Trumbo (1996) has more recently analyzed global warming from a Downsian perspective as well.

events that attracted social attention. He noted that global warming evidence was available for quite some time before the enormous increase in interest to the warming issue occurring in 1988. In Ungar's view, only the construction of a "social scare," precipitated by the real-world "concatenating physical impacts" of the drought of 1988, brought global warming into view as a legitimate threat to personal well-being (p. 490). This social scare brought demand for news to which both print and broadcast news media attended. These stories "fed" on each other, leading to enormous increases in media coverage. For Ungar, the global warming attention cycle expired because of the inability to sustain a sense of dramatic crisis over the environmental issue. In this case, the extreme temperatures and drought conditions of the summer of 1988 focused public attention on global warming, essentially giving it "celebrity" status. When those events are transient, as weather certainly is, the event's notoriety fades, the issue appears to be less of a social problem, and public attention moves on to other issues. Thus, public attentiveness to environmental claims increases when those claims "piggyback" on actual events that force the issues into the public consciousness, and decreases when competing events replace them in the headlines.

Whereas Ungar viewed issue cycles as catalyzed by actual events (in this case, the hot 1988 summer), and Hilgartner and Bosk focused on the social factors that attract or detract attention from an issue, we would pay more attention to how the news media construct narratives about the issue. Within a narrative framework, we think both a realist and a social perspective can coexist. Even real-world events must be submitted to a dramatic retelling (as Downs also implicitly recognized) to make for the social scare that Ungar described.

As seen in chapter 3, a comprehensive literature has examined how narratives influence our worldview. We also argued that societal dependence on media narratives is especially important in cases involving environmental issues, such as ozone depletion or global climate change, where the mass media assist people in understanding obscure yet potentially threatening situations in terms of their everyday lives. Translating "issues" and "phenomena" into meaningful "stories" essentially involves dramatic considerations (i.e., how to portray issues in the most vivid, affecting manner possible). These include decisions about storyline, actors, and themes, which take into account the shared social realities of storyteller and audience. As Jacobs (1996) observed in his study on narratives used by broadcasters, "News work is not merely an instrumental task of 'filling the news hole'. . . . [It] requires the transformation of discrete events into meaningful narratives" (pp. 392-393).

For Bormann (1982, 1985), meaningful narratives use "fantasy themes" to create a social reality for audiences. The appearance of group consciousness is therefore an outcome not so much of individual experiences but of shared social experiences through common narratives or fantasies. Gronbeck (1983) also argued that meaningfulness is created through a shared set of "symbol systems" by the storyteller and the audience. At times, media construction of meaning leads to a shared set of misconstruals among lay audiences. Bell (1994) maintained, for instance, that media discourse on global climate change in New Zealand did not adequately relate the causes of the climate condition nor distinguish it from ozone depletion to the public. As a result, he believes the public may not be equipped to deal with the causes of global pollution.

Some of these narrative concepts are evident in research on media coverage of science and environmental issues, such as the emphasis on drama and sensational events. Mazur and Lee (1993), for instance, found that in most cases, human drama rather than science played the primary role in an environmental story's coming to the media's attention; some issues, such as the ozone hole, gained coverage months after their discoveries. Thematic decisions can also result in a dampening of interest in an environmental issue. Wilkins and Patterson (1991), in their examination of newspaper coverage of global climate change in 1987 and 1988, found a shift from a science-oriented to a policy-oriented framework. In turn, they argued that global warming eventually disappeared from the media's agenda because no clear political symbol was attached to it.

Yet, the storytellers themselves operate under the implicit social constraints of news organizations, and "dramatic" decisions will likely vary depending on the organization. Jacobs (1996) observed that broadcast news stations operate narratively at each step of news production: when stories are "discovered" and conceptualized as being part of a larger plot; when narratives are used to legitimate the story's newsworthiness to the news director, and when stories are told to the audience.

Pertaining to the environment, Nimmo and Combs (1982) examined television network news coverage of Three Mile Island and found that the dramatic emphasis differed by network, reflecting various decision-making procedures, audience preferences, and institutional ethos of the organizations. In another study of television coverage of environmental risk, Greenberg et al. (1989) found that networks were more influenced by the story's dramatic value than the issue's inherent risk. Finally, Wilkins (1993) examined the underlying values of print media coverage of global warming from 1987 to 1990 and found that they included U.S. notions of progress, the institution of knowledge in scientific and governmental bodies, and innocence. Wilkins argued that these values reflect the dominant frame that emphasizes technological "fixes" for environmental problems over human behavior changes.

What emerges from this research is how important narratives are to news story construction. Thus, we ask whether narratives about global warming change over time, and if they correspond in some narrative way to the stages of Downs' issue-attention cycle: preproblem, alarmed discovery, and so forth. Research has already documented rises and falls in quantity of coverage resembling a Downsian cycle in print and broadcast media coverage of global climate change in the late 1980s (Mazur & Lee, 1993; Trumbo, 1994, 1996; Ungar, 1992). In this chapter, we present a both a graphical analysis (to show how the cycle has progressed in years not covered by previous studies) and an examination of the narrative structure of national news media coverage of global climate change between 1980 and 1994.

METHODS

To gain empirical perspective on cyclical news coverage of global climate change, we first examined a sample of national news coverage from 1980 to 1994 to discover whether a Downsian cycle did occur. Research has shown that media coverage, including both print and broadcast, of global climate change peaked in the late 1980s; anecdotal evidence and our own research suggests that media attention dropped drastically in the 1990s.

A detailed analysis of the coverage required narrowing our media search. As our database, we used the indices of *The New York Times* and *The Washington Post*, both national newspapers of record. For both newspapers, we recorded the frequency of stories listed under "global warming" or "greenhouse effect." In the case of *The Times*, global warming stories, identifiable by their abstracts, were also listed under "weather." Figure 6.1 presents data for frequency of global climate change coverage in *The Times* and *The Post*.

The figure was prepared by calculating the number of stories that, at any given data point, had appeared in the last 5 months in both papers. From this number, a 5-month moving average was calculated to smooth data fluctuations.

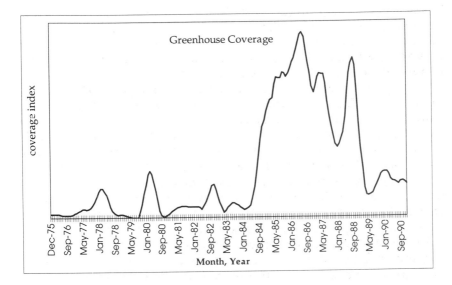

Figure 6.1. Trend in newspaper coverage of global warming in *The New York Times* and *The Washington Post*

ANATOMY OF THE COVERAGE

Some previous research has given interesting summaries of greenhouse coverage (e.g., Bell, 1994; Mazur & Lee, 1993). We offer a skeletal summary of major developments here because the later date of our analysis allows us to consider "backlash" developments that are only now becoming evident and that contribute to the development of theory.

Downs stated that in the preproblem stage, an undesirable condition exists but has not captured much public attention, even though some groups may already be alarmed by it. Early coverage of global climate change illustrates this stage. For instance, in 1983, *The Times* ran the story of the report issued by the National Academy of Sciences, warning of a build up in carbon gases in the atmosphere. The report was dismissed by a Reagan administration scientist as being "alarmist," and the issue went away for some years (Shabecoff, 1983).

In 1986, Dr. James Hansen, a NASA scientist, went out on a limb and definitively concluded that the greenhouse effect was taking place, a position reported in a June 11 story in *The New York Times*. Although predictions of a global temperature rise were included, no dire consequences were specifically mentioned in the story. However, the report suggested that greenhouse gas accumulation was speeding up (Shabecoff, 1986). These early reports were cautious and straightforward and not associated with any definitive rise in overall coverage trends or public concern, much in tune with Downs' hypothesis. Then, starting in 1988, stories began to acquire a more strident, and even desperate, tone.

An explosion in coverage clearly occurred around 1988 (see Figure 6.1). From a Downsian perspective, this represents the alarmed discovery and euphoric enthusiasm stage, when due to some dramatic events, the public suddenly becomes aware of the social condition and soon after becomes ardent about society's ability to "solve this problem" (Downs, 1972, p. 39). Yet, as discussed previously, the graphical data show that the problem had actually been "discovered" earlier. This suggests that knowledge alone is not enough to "construct" the alarm on which Downs' hypothesis rests, confirming Ungar's analysis as well. Ungar argued that this 1988 increase was catalyzed by the hot summer and drought. But we surmise that in order to produce the alarm Downs predicted, stories must emphasize dangers inherent in the problem and be perceived as actually representing a danger (not every issue gets such coverage in the media, and fewer get the audience response eventually received by climate issues). Thus, we argue that the choice of social construction lies in the narrative decision to portray a hot summer as harbinger of global disaster, as opposed to framing the event as a natural perturbation in weather patterns, for example.

Many news sources reported that the hottest years in recent memory had all occurred in the 1980s. In particular, the very hot U.S. summer of 1988 lent credence to a developing feeling that the world itself was becoming noticeably hotter. Popular media reported this very widely, magnifying the effect of a few scientific reports. These factual reports, mostly from sources such as the EPA and the National Academy of Sciences, increasingly began to be interspersed with poorly founded speculative predictions of the possible effects of such warming, especially reports of the possible impact of polar ice melting and a resultant increase in ocean levels. These disaster "hooks" offered news persons a way to give the greenhouse story relevance in personal and social life. Rather than an esoteric issue of marginal scientific interest, global warming acquired a storyline that could be easily manipulated. Metaphors and scene setting increasingly reflected disaster. For example, Jeremy Rifkin, writing in *The Post* on July 31, 1988, constructed the following scenario:

> The year is 2035. In New York, palm trees line the Hudson River from 125th to the Midtown exit.

> Phoenix is in its third week of temperatures over 130 degrees, and the project to cover the city with air-conditioned domes is still unfinished.
>
> Holland is under water. Bangladesh has ceased to exist. Torrential rains and rising seas there have killed several million people and forced the remaining population into makeshift refugee camps on higher ground in Pakistan and India.
>
> Welcome to the Greenhouse World of the 21st century. (p. C3)

During the next two years, *The Times* and *The Post* reported scientific developments, often alongside imagery of doomsday predictions similar to those of Rifkin. In retrospect, we can see that in the face of impending global disaster, among experts nothing was certain, other than uncertainty, yet many accounts leaned toward the worst-case scenario. *The New York Times* reporter Philip Shabecoff (1988a) wrote that "experts predict major changes in climatic patterns and a gradual rise in sea levels as the warming oceans expand and polar ice melts. Coastal flooding, dust bowls, sharply reduced crops, and dying forests could result in some regions. On the other hand, relatively barren areas might become farmlands" (p. 1). Another example we find typical of this period's coverage is a story published in *The Times* on June 26, 1988:

> According to some of the most dire predictions, this is how bad a summer day might be in the year 2030:
>
> The temperature in Washington, DC is over 100 degrees for the 10th straight day. Air conditioners are running at maximum around the clock, straining the generating capacity of electrical power plants and assuring another jump in already soaring utility rates.
>
> In New York City, heat is not the only problem. Workers are raising levees to hold back the rising tidal waters of the Hudson and East rivers.
>
> In the south, another 100,000 acres of Louisiana wetland is being lost to the sea. But Chicago is suffering from another extreme. Evaporation has been causing Lake Michigan to recede from Lake Shore Drive, leaving behind an ever widening expanse of malodorous mud. (Shabecoff, 1988b, p. 1)

Not all stories were doomsday in nature, but scientific accounts, inevitably cautious in nature, were quickly overwhelmed in other media (as suggested by Trumbo's analysis) by the lurid predictions. For instance, *The Post* reporter Philip Hilts, covering the Second North American Conference on Preparing for Climate Change, composed the following lead:

Disease-carrying parasites swarming up from the tropics and soft clams disappearing from the Chesapeake Bay are among the dislocations and disturbances that scientists say are possible results of a long-term warming trend that they agree is taking place. (p. A4)

Only two paragraphs later does the reader learn that confirmation of these predictions may not be possible for several years.

In stories such as this, where hazardous consequences and marginally probable outcomes are the focus, the "reality" of global warming, a topic notorious for its reliance on computer-modeled data built on many assumptions, was simply assumed, with no clear estimate of the probability of warming firmly established in the public mind (although a warming of about 3 to 8 degrees during the next 50 years was mentioned most frequently). Although *The Times* and *The Post* reporters certainly practiced responsible journalism, seeking countervailing opinions from a variety of sources, we think that these forms of coverage established near-term public expectations, such as visible rises in sea level, more extreme weather, and continued and noticeable warming trends, that could not be met. Thus, when North American weather turned drastically colder in the next few years (probably due to particulate spew from Mount Pinatubo), it was no surprise when people began to see the earlier predictions as pseudoscientific hokum.

For Downs, the rise in greenhouse coverage would be seen merely as a "natural" public discovery of a particular environmental problem. For Ungar, the unusually warm temperatures of 1988 facilitated the factual claims-making and media activities that create social scare phenomena. For Hilgartner and Bosk, feedback from claims-making activities in public arenas, such as the media or Congress, results in the problem gaining widespread attention in many arenas. From our perspective, however, the narrative dimension in media coverage is as important, especially because some factual knowledge of the greenhouse problem significantly predated the increase in concern. We see media coverage as narratively constructing the rapid increase in alarmism associated with the issues.

This alarmism was actively built in story choice and presentation; it was not simply a feature of the issue itself. In retrospect, it seems more than just a particular scientific problem or real-world event was needed; a story with specific, dangerous, and visually imaginable consequences, with someone willing to verify its truth, was necessary. But for global climate change, raised expectations of danger and disaster obviously would not materialize in the short term. Given that, it is not surprising that the bubble burst in the early 1990s.

Downs asserted that issue attention declines due to public realization of the cost of solving the problem. Ungar cited "demand attenuation" as a fairly natural form of declining attention for issues and issue agendas. Hilgartner and Bosk pointed to other factors, such as "carrying capacities," competition for media space, and need for sustained drama, that influence attention decline. We agree with these reasons, particularly with Hilgartner and Bosk's emphasis on the need for sustained drama. Predictions of disaster become strident and shrill in the short term; there is little long-term narrative energy to cover disaster predictions that do not come "true." Over the long term, such predictions will discourage attention for the issue, much as the fabled shepherd boy who cried "wolf" too many times.

As it becomes clear that disaster may not occur within the short term, narrative logic demands another motor to drive the story. At this point, news stories about global warming began to deal with the "debate" about the issue. Inevitably, political debate establishes doubts about the reality or importance of the problem. Therefore, once the press has established expectations of doom and disaster that cannot be met, the political aspects of the story, the conflictual aspects, must emerge as a way to sustain dramatic interest. In the case of global warming, these stories emerge particularly (although not exclusively) on the "downside" of the attention cycle.

In the context of global warming, this meant a turn to White House skepticism on the issue. President George Bush and his advisor John Sununu, in particular, afforded journalists a way to reframe the global warming issue in a more interesting, dramatic, and conflictual way. Thus, stories began to focus more and more frequently on political, social, and economic debate. Consequences were less frequently mentioned, and when discussed were thrown more into question.

The late 1980s had set up an atmosphere in which greenhouse warming was an imminent disaster. The level of early 1990s' coverage, and the yearly growth in such coverage, could only have been maintained by an outcome that actually matched predictions. With the turn of the decade, a variety of "outside" forces conspired to reduce attention to the problem. Although Bush had campaigned as an "environmental president," his attention to such issues was minimal. The Persian Gulf War and economic woes further seemed to divert media and public attention away from the problem of global climate change. Indeed, in the face of Middle Eastern enemies and rapidly escalating economic problems, the predictions of just two years earlier acquired an almost comic or nostalgic character. The 1992 United Nations Conference on Environment and Development, the so-called "Earth Summit," provided one last hurrah for greenhouse coverage in the national press. When President Bush signed an emasculated international agreement, the national press seemed willing to accept that as the final word on the issue, as is evident by the rapid decrease in print media coverage of global climate change. Record snow and cold in the nation's decision-making centers merely confirmed the wisdom of this approach.

More than that, the early narrative enthusiasm for dire greenhouse predictions fueled the eventual backlash. Stevens, in *The Times* on September 14, 1993, discussed the attempt of scientists to counter the characterization of global warming as an hysterical "flash in the pan" (p. 1). Yet, given the nature of the dramatic coverage, it is perhaps not surprising that this characterization has met with increasing acceptance. Indeed, many environmental issues have experienced a measured stepping back from the criticisms offered in the late 1980s (e.g., radon, ozone depletion). From a public opinion standpoint, a corollary result has been a drop in concern for and attention to environmental issues (Moore, 1995).

Indeed, as Stevens reported, the

> rhetoric is the mirror image of some that was heard five years ago, at the height of the North American heat wave, when some environmentalists and politicians warned of climatic apocalypse on the basis of assertions by a minority of scientists that global warming was already under way. (p. 1)

That the rhetoric is indeed a mirror image speaks volumes. Although the intended argument of the new backlash rhetoric may be the reverse of that seen five years ago, its narrative style is not radically different. A pendular swing from one position to its polar opposite is the end result. In five short years, global warming's "imminent disaster" had become the cranky forecast of socialist-environmental "wackos."

DISCUSSION

A theory of issue-attention cycles needs to account for more than just the qualities of issues themselves. Narrative must be accounted for, as the discussion here suggests. Media structural factors must also be taken into account. What has not been rigorously analyzed is how institutional media constraints contribute to these construals. We think it is clear that potentially disastrous outcomes make for better ratings and circulation numbers. Also, in a situation where a narrative critical mass is developing, press reports will tend to reinforce each other, producing the commonsense impression that the problem is important, "in the now," and worthy of immediate attention. We speculate that this choice of presentation is what happened with global climate change around 1988. Thus, the piggybacking Ungar described is more than just a reporting of unusual events: It is a narrative choice to present them as highly and impendingly dangerous.

Wilkins and Patterson (1991) contended that global warming did not receive sustained media coverage because it failed to reach a symbolic threshold in the political debate. Their study does not cover the entire cycle as we do. Although not disagreeing with their conclusions, we would argue that the political debate itself played a role in the decline in attention and media coverage. Once the conflictual aspects and uncertainty surrounding global climate change science began appearing more and more in the newspapers—concurrently with reports on political debates—the reinforcement of the dramatic crescendo in coverage began to wither.

We suggest a corollary to Downs' hypothesis. In cases where media construct environmental issues as imminently threatening, public attention to the issue will not be sustained unless those predictions themselves can be substantiated. We also hypothesize that the periodicity of the cycle (i.e., how long it takes to rise and fall), will be directly proportionate to the damages, consequences, and risks inherent in the predictions. In other words, more threatening predictions will result in faster increases and decreases in attention if the predictions do not come true in the short term. Although perhaps only relevant to environmental issues, the hypothesis, if true, would show more directly why attention to some issues increases and then decreases rapidly.

This "Chicken Little" argument goes a long way toward explaining current public dissatisfaction with environmental issues. Because environmental destruction has not resulted from global climate change (at least in any immediately evident way), the logic of public opinion and news narratives suggests that those presenting the idea were wrong or sensationalizing the problem in the first place. Our corollary offers a directly testable proposition, something Downs' theory really does not give.

SHORT TERM CYCLES AS COMPONENTS OF LONGER TERM TRENDS

We have seen that, from 1980 to 1994, the media attended to the issue of global warming in a cyclical way. Compared to the long-term environmental cycle observed in Figure 5.1, the ups and downs of issue attention to global warming came pretty quickly. What effect does the relatively "rapid" increase and decrease of issue attention in newspapers have on longer term relationships between news exposure and adherence to environmental beliefs? Do these rapid boom-bust cycles increase attention and adherence to environmentalist beliefs, or do people become fed up with such shenanigans and ignore the issue entirely?

To answer these questions requires a return to narrative thinking. Each environmental story, posing a potential disaster, attracts viewers because of its "sensational" portent of world-consuming conflagration. But it would be problematic to judge news impacts on environmental belief only from one story. Since the late 1960s, a series of environmental stories have also, in some sense, been covered cyclically. These stories, strung together, form part of a larger news narrative; perhaps we can think of this as an environmental meta-narrative (and this gets us closer to thinking about the environmental master story we spoke of in earlier chapters). Thus, global warming, although an important story, was only one among many that were covered with more frequency in progression from about 1970. Figure 6.2 shows how a variety of selected issues were also covered in a generally cyclical pattern since the late 1980s. This figure was also prepared by looking at indices from *The New York Times* and *The Washington Post*; the figure shows that most issues received increased attention around the years from 1989 to 1991, corresponding to the time during which global warming received attention.

This shows the action of a wider environmental narrative operating in newspaper coverage of the environmental issue. Although newspapers began to give greater credence to the environmental beat in the late 1980s, institutional steps toward more effective environmental coverage resulted in greater attention to the issue across a broad range of topics (this is evident in the graph for across-issue coverage totals in Figure 6.2). Although not every issue's coverage pattern displays a truly cyclical pattern, it is quite evident that coverage of specific issues was motivated by an underlying general tendency toward increasing frequency of coverage for environmental issues. Around 1990, that was good news for the proponents of news media as encouragers of environmental concern.

Yet, both Figures 6.1 and 6.2 show decreases in attention to environmental issues after about 1992. Although a decline in global warming issue coverage accounts for much of the overall decline, other issues received less attention as well. Acid rain, the other blockbuster issue of the 1980s, began its decline before the late 1980s (see Figure 6.3) but other issues received less attention in the early 1990s.

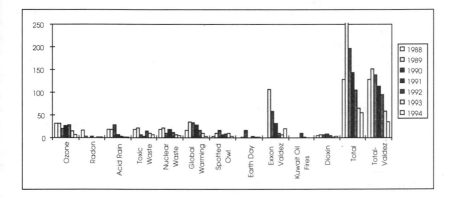

**Figure 6.2. Patterns of coverage for various environmental issues
in The New York Times (1988-1992)**

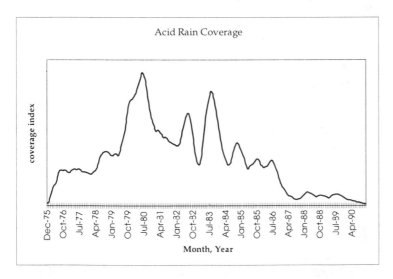

**Figure 6.3. Trend in newspaper coverage of acid rain in The New
York Times and The Washington Post**

For instance, theories of ozone depletion appeared in the mid-1970s, but widescale recognition did not come for another decade when scientists recorded an "ozone hole" over Antarctica larger than the United States. Media coverage rapidly increased during the mid- to late 1980s, spurred on by international negotiations for the Montreal Protocol in 1987. The Protocol called for a 50% reduction in the production of chlorofluorocarbons and other ozone-depleting chemicals. Media coverage peaked in 1988 and 1989, and despite a brief resurgence in 1991 following the release of an EPA study, coverage continued its downward trend. We think the dramatic image of an ozone "hole" (although hole is perhaps not an appropriate term to apply to the phenomenon) is what made ozone an attractive issue from a narrative perspective.

Radon is another environmental issue that illustrates Downs' cycle. Radon came into the national headlines in January 1988, when the National Academy of Sciences blamed radon for 13,000 new cases of lung cancer each year. Moreover, the threat came from an odorless, colorless gas that naturally collected in people's homes. In light of these reports, the government issued a nationwide public health advisory urging people to test their homes for radon. After extended media coverage in 1988, however, radon received only minimal coverage in 1989, illustrating one of the greatest drops in coverage of a theoretically ongoing environmental concern. More recent stories state that some scientists think the radon threat was "overblown." Radon's narrative positioning as a mysterious and deadly gas was undoubtedly important to its prominence in environmental coverage patterns.

Also in the 1980s, the northern spotted owl became a prominent environmental issue that also demonstrated cyclical properties. Media coverage of the spotted owl debate peaked in 1989, as the debate centered around people who opposed and those who supported continued logging in the ancient, old-growth forests of the Pacific Northwest. At issue were an estimated 10,000 to 28,000 logging jobs potentially lost over the next decade versus the estimated 3,600 pairs of spotted owls that inhabit the forests. Media coverage declined after 1990, when the government formally declared the spotted owl a "threatened species," which made destroying its critical habitat illegal. Not only did the spotted owl symbolize narratively interesting conflicts between environmental enemies, it also suggested the sinister possibility of critical loss of global biodiversity.

We think these examples show the boundaries of the environmental meta-narrative that developed through the late 1980s. Although specific issues and their attendant dangers provided a certain narrative kind of energy, the interaction between these issues and their perceptions in readers' minds must undoubtedly also have been important. Thus, in a world with a multiplicity of dangerous and mysterious environmental phenomena that threaten us, the appearance of any single new issue gains more credence as an important problem. The environmental news feeding frenzy that got under way in 1988 was, we think, working on this general model.

Thus, it is perhaps not surprising that the meta-narrative collapsed in the same way as did the global warming narrative: Coverage of each issue, promising or threatening impending disaster (due to narrative construction) was eventually forced to reflect the fact that promised environmental dangers were not occurring. Once this fact became evident in the meta-narrative, a watershed point was reached, and the narrative demand for stories about the environment in the news marketplace receded. In a sense, the environmental news market "crashed."

This argument suggests that attention to print news probably does not result in greater long-term adherence to environmentalist positions on environmental issues. It certainly gives little hope that news media will be useful for long-term paradigmatic change. To examine this question, we again turned to GSS data to see whether newspaper readership was associated with greater environmentalism and how such associations may have varied over time. Figure 6.4 shows how GSS respondents, characterized by

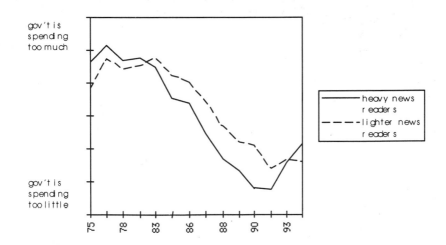

Figure 6.4. Trends in support for environmental spending, by news readership (1975-1994)

either frequent or light newspaper readership, responded to the GSS question about support for governmental environmental spending previously analyzed in chapter 5.

The figure shows that frequent news readers did "lead" less frequent news readers in their growth of support for governmental environmental spending. This can probably be interpreted as an agenda-setting effect of environmental news coverage and its growth throughout the 1980s. Thus, at least in the 1980s, news coverage did appear to produce support for a move toward new paradigm environmental thinking.

Yet, when the meta-narrative collapsed in the early 1990s, evident also is that more frequent newsreaders were quick to lead the pack back toward a less environmentally concerned position. The frequency of coverage of issues such as the "brownlash" and the prominence of writers such as Greg Easterbrook, Julian Simon, and others shows that press attention and its effects may behave cyclically even at the meta-narrative level.

Thus, both newspaper coverage and television attention to environmental issues behave in cyclical ways. Of course, our data only cover one cyclical period; it may be that in the future we will observe noncyclical patterns. In any case, a negative can never be proven, so noncyclical patterns could logically emerge. Still, the apparent correlations between patterns of news coverage and entertainment and their effects support our arguments that media institutions (including quality newspapers such as *The Times* and *The Post*) should not be seen as in the vanguard of a putative move toward a new environmental paradigm. In the next and final chapter, we try to summarize our position on the wider issues of media environmentalism.

seven

DO NARRATIVES
MATTER?

The radio and the telephone
And the movies that we know
May just be passing fancies
And in time may go . . .
—Ira Gershwin

In the previous chapters, we depicted several dimensions of the complex relationship between media portrayals of the environment, people's beliefs about the environment, and actual environmental states. In this chapter, we attempt to unify these perspectives into a somewhat more comprehensive theoretical perspective on media and the environment.

Many previous works on media and the environment have implicitly accepted the assumption that, because media can disseminate information effectively, they should also be expected to promote environmental conservation and better understanding of environmental issues. This goes along with the fairly pervasive assumption that, historically, we should attribute environmental progress since the 1960s, at least in part, to media attention.

Only a few authors have questioned these assumptions; Mander (1991) and McKibben (1992) are two. Arguing from a markedly more critical social perspective, they suggested that television and its media cousins are causally "responsible" for environmental degradation, as opposed to somehow being indirectly involved with environmental improvement. Our own arguments, coming from a more traditional social science perspective, are among the only empirical demonstrations of the potential validity of these ideas. Although Mander and McKibben deploy powerful polemics in favor of their positions, their tendency to fly rhetorical argument on scant combustible fuel is problematic. That is one of the reasons we chose an empirical path in the latter chapters of this book, although the choice opens up problems of its own. But Mander's and McKibben's more visionary approach to the problem more than makes up for their excesses. Our own feeling is that critical positions such as those advanced by McKibben and Mander should be "demonstrated" empirically, insofar as they can. Our attempt in this book has been to bridge the critical and the empirical communication perspectives on environmental issues in a way that can provide a more convincing rationale for social action.

Of course, complex social phenomena will not always easily reduce to numerical facts. In the end, even our quantitative analyses rest on our own interpretation of environmental texts, and we recognize that. Still, we see important connections between our empirical results and our narrative theorizing.

In Chapter 1, we suggest that our society is experiencing an ongoing attempt to engage with the environment in a way that does not place too much weight on the structural members of the dominant social paradigm. We suggest seeing that as a kind of narrative struggle. Despite our clearly critical position on media's contributions to environmental beliefs, we feel that one can discern the outlines of a legitimate and organic environmental dialogue that struggles to emerge into the mainstream discourse. The "grassroots" dialogue on environmental issues has increasingly made an important contribution to environmental progress, and even the mass media sporadically make important contributions to an environmental discourse that bears an intelligent relationship to the environment it discusses. And we agree that, overall, we find ourselves in a healthier environmental position than where we were 5, 10, and 25 years ago. Improvements in air quality, water quality, and in other environmental areas are undoubtedly a partial outcome of the environmental discourse that has successfully problematized these issues. Even though media institutions are structured so as to facilitate a hegemonic form of social control, we stipulate that there appears to be significant room for "leakage" of productive environmental discourse. That is, social control by media institutions is not completely effective.

However, we think it is fundamentally wrong to give "primary" credit to media institutions for environmental progress, as so much of the research has suggested should or could be the case. Indeed, we argue that in the environmental sphere as in other spheres, mass media tend to attach themselves to social trends after the trends have achieved mainstream attention and legitimacy; similarly, media tend to get off social movement bandwagons before social vanguards. Although media may certainly play some role in disseminating ideas about social change to wider audiences, we think it is just as true that media tend to keep their most attentive audiences closer to the social mainstream. That is, the media propagandize in a subtle way for the status quo. Insofar as environmentalism has been a specifically anti-status quo social movement, it follows that mainstream commercial mass media are, in some sense, anti-environmental.

We realize this contradicts commonsense experience. Especially during the late 1980s and early 1990s, it seemed that media were very much in the forefront of promoting attention to environmental issues. Similarly, it appeared that the corporate structure behind media institutions was learning to take a greener approach. Examples abound: Hollywood's fascination with Earth Day and other environmental issues, McDonald's decision to move away from styrofoam packaging, the proliferation of children's shows focusing on environmental issues, and many other similar examples of media environmentalism all suggested that the environmental social movement had finally achieved some mainstream legitimacy. And indeed, it would be hard to disagree with this assessment, but we must ask, at what price was this legitimacy gained?

To some extent, we are tempted to conclude that the media environmental discourse so popular in the late 1980s was a narrative attempt on the part of both audiences and media to substitute for a more organically sustainable environmental dialogue. That is, we think that the media discourse worked as a kind of "stand-in" for a more real encounter with environmental issues. We might term this a *para-natural* interaction (borrowing from the theorists who talk about television as providing para-social interaction). Television's nature programs, environmental humor, sporadic and cyclical attention to environmental problems in the news, and separation of environmental themes from other topics all suggest that the television discourse lacked the genuine quality that would support the argument that television and other mass media can provide a true engagement with environmental issues. Thus, we conclude along with both Mander and McKibben, although from a different evidence base, that television and other dominant media institutions can be seen as an essentially anti-environmental force.

To review, Mander saw TV as an anti-environmental force because of the extreme differences manifested between the "artificial" culture of television and the "authentic" culture of Native Americans (whom he saw as reflecting a "correct" environmental ideology). To a certain extent we agree with Mander, although we have argued that simplistic views of Native culture as more environmentally "authentic" than others are not necessarily helpful. Still, Mander's anecdotal evidence from Native Americans who encounter television (he found that television tends to accelerate the "destruction" of Native American culture) is somewhat congruent with our evidence that television's messages maintain the dominant status quo in the societies where they organically and originally developed. Thus, although television radically changes traditional cultures, its main effect in Western society is to preserve the moral and social order. In a sense, its main effect is that there is no effect. Mander, who has essentially argued that television damages authentic cultures because of its consumerist content, finds a powerful confirmation of his ideas in our data.

> Television is uniquely suited to implant and continuously reinforce dominant ideologies. And, while it hones our minds, it also accelerates our nervous systems into a form that matches the technological reality that is upon us. Television effectively produces a new form of human being—less creative, less able to make subtle distinctions, speedier, and more interested in things—albeit better able to handle, appreciate, approve of the new technological world. (p. 96)

On the other hand, McKibben presented a more nuanced argument suggesting that a medium such as television can never present a truly authentic environmental discourse precisely because it is a technologically mediated form of experience. Although our data do not address this question directly, we suggest that the very powerful combination of form and content makes television such an efficient machine for maintaining the DSP. No other system has the potential for so powerfully removing and distancing us from the environment while imbuing our narrative memory with messages designed so subtly to make real a world of entirely social design. But McKibben argued that escape from this mediated social reality is not so difficult.

I grew up rapt with attention at the words and the images on the screen. Darren and Gilligan and Mrs. Brady and Peter Jennings and all the rest—this was the real world. I assumed unconsciously that the information that poured from the TV into my quite similar suburban world was all the information there was, except for stuff about sex, which back then they couldn't show. But there's another real world. A realer world, maybe—certainly an older one. This world is full of information, information that grows inevitably in you the more time you spend there, the stiller you are. (pp. 248-249)

Television presents a powerful *pseudoenvironment.* The term was first used by Lippmann (1922), who so powerfully saw that no reality could escaped unprocessed in a world dominated by symbol systems and the media. Lippmann argued that pseudoenvironments, the construction of elite symbolizing institutions, would eventually come to stand in as reality for "real" environments, and thus motivate people to action. But Lippmann never argued that the actual physical environment could ever be subsumed within a mediated construction. Only recently have more radical authors such as Evernden come to this position. Although we argued this is technically not possible (for reasons of systemic complexity), we think that television clearly represents a very important institution drawing narrative force from the natural environment.

Since Chapter 1, we have seen that television's pervasive consistency in matters of the environment does have measurable impacts with respect to social change. Although we are constrained by rather primitive measures of adherence to the NEP, television's role clearly is to slow environmental change when it is heading away from the moderate center favored by the DSP and to accelerate change when it is heading back to that center. Thus, the moral of television's environmental story is that the more things don't change the more they stay the same. As Gitlin (1982) persuasively argued, when thinking about the effects of mass media, to think about ways in which media help maintain the status quo may be most correct.

Still, on a somewhat shallower level, exposure to news messages is associated with an accelerating support for social change on environmental issues, at least at certain points in news cycles. As our coverage of the global warming issue shows, however, this acceleration comes at a price: When an environmental bubble bursts, there is a concomitant drop in attention for the issue, and a catastrophic failure in the market for attention to the issue may ensue. As we have shown, narratives and narrative styles play an important role in the environmental cycle that Downs identified so

early on. Thus, even legitimate and dangerous environmental problems are subject to the ups and downs of environmental narratives
that rely on scare tactics and sensationalism. In the end, we think
this probably encourages a sense of futility when thinking about
environmental problems. Indeed, as our data show, attention to
media narratives tends to result in less commitment to solving
environmental issues on some dimensions, and it appears that fear
constructs are very much involved in this phenomenon.

We also argue that fictional and nonfictional messages on
the environment probably "go together" and reinforce each other in
some interesting ways. We give more weight to fictional messages,
which we think attack the deeper level (the level of the social environment) by creating, recreating, and maintaining dominant conceptions of the environment. We have seen that, in fictional programming, the environment tends to be both symbolically annihilat-
ed and disconnected from "foregrounded" lifestyle concerns that are
the prime topics of television entertainment. This powerful narrative
weight draws the conceptions of viewers toward the social center,
where they can be exploited by the social elites controlling television
and other media industries. This exploitation comes in the lessened
demand for social change that certainly results from the deadening
of the weight that pushes for environmental progress. In cultivation
terms, this mainstreaming is the most noticeable and important
environmental effect from exposure to television messages.

We see several kinds of functions for this narrative system.
For the audience, the functions have been adequately evaluated by
numerous scholars who have shown why audiences find solace and
satisfaction in their media products. The audience practices and
principles associated with modern U.S. entertainment media are
basically well understood: People want a belief system (secular consumerism), and they want a return for their attention to media
products and willingness to consume advertising (entertainment).
Nothing perverse or subversive is in these desires, which the media
play on successfully precisely because such desires seem eminently
natural within the boundaries of the DSP. Although much of our
argument suggests that the media serve as a kind of machine to
reproduce and maintain the DSP, that the mass media could not
have been built as presently structured without the previous existence of the DSP is also the case: Modern media practices assume
the DSP as a foundational building block; without the DSP modern
media practices would not make sense. So, in a sense, there is a
reciprocal and symbiotic relationship between the media and hegemonic social conceptions of the environment.

For social elites, we think the most important and generally
underrecognized environmental function is one of social control. As

argued in chapter 3, modern media institutions play a social control function through repetitive exposure of mass audiences to messages consonant with the desires of social elites that control the mass media. At the ideological level, the level of the social environment, we think that media institutions' messages contribute to the maintenance of the status quo. At the level of the social construction of the environment, we think that media institutions, while attracting attention to particular issues, tend to dissuade audiences that they can or should play a role in solving environmental problems. With global warming, the frantic ups and downs of coverage can be linked to audience disconnectedness from these problems as issues that have direct relationships to everyday lifestyle practices. Although news stories on global warming emphasized scientific uncertainty and portents of doom, one could argue that the most important aspect of the story (the relationship between global consumption and pollutants that contribute to global warming) was basically ignored. From the perspective of the elite institutions dependent on the DSP, then, news messages play a valuable role: They attract "attention" for environmental issues without challenging the basic tenets of the DSP. That is, as we suggested at the beginning of the book, they begin to create a narrative in which tentative connections are made to thinking about the natural environment in ways that do not motivate social change. Thus, although media cannot be accused of "ignoring" problems, their attention to the issues seems to have little positive effect.

The proliferation of references to the natural environment in our media products is another example of the process by which we establish nonthreatening ways to think about the environment and environmental problems without challenging the dicta of the DSP. Is it so surprising that from 1988 to 1992, the height of news media hysteria on environmental problems, an entire commercial culture arose based on environmental imagery and supposedly environmentally friendly products? Nature programs, nature stores, nature music, and so on were evidence of a very active commercial culture based on exploiting a very real desire to experience a connection with the natural world. In the end, however, nature turns out to be a fashion much like short skirts or disco. Within a few short years, we may look nostalgically back at our period of nature infatuation in the same way that we fondly remember poodle skirts or swing music.

We argue that this surface environmental discourse is one in which environmental issues have been characterized as problems that can be solved essentially within the rubric of the DSP. When large problems such as global warming tend to disappear and the smaller ones are solved by implementing a few shifts in corporate practice, the ultimate lesson is that things work well under the current social system. From this perspective, finally, we see the media discourse as an ideologically tinged fiction useful insofar as it has allowed us to participate in a narrative version of an environment in which we can make real and meaningful change in a universe of higher certainty.

In this paranatural universe of discourse, our decision to recycle a soda can is a decision that counts. Our decision to take eco-tourist vacations is another decision that counts. Do these decisions lead to measurable and real environmental impacts? We argue that the effects are negligible. But such decisions play a very important role in the way we build an environmental narrative; they are decisions that hang together well in a system of narrative rationality that allows us to deal with environmental issues without a radical social critique.

We also think that this narrative system tends to "block" movement toward an organically real NEP. Although the concept of the NEP is an attractive and hopeful vision of an environmental future, we do not see that current mass discourse shows any real evidence of moving toward a more real connection to the actual natural environment.

Is this a conspiracy? Of course not, because we are talking about a social system that is not under the control of a few individuals. But we can see the system as one that has evolved because it works. That is, the system serves the logic of the technocratic, capitalist entertainment state that has, in an unprecedented way, proven its ability to attract the ideological and practical adherence of most of its members. Individuals gain from this massive attention to their individual needs: One's senses are gratified, and one can be gratified at will. At the same time, this attention serves the needs of advertisers and others who depend on this attention for making their own way in the world. As one hand washes the others, one can hardly dispute that the system has its own logic and even appeal. So what is the problem?

One comes back to the issue of the gravity imposed on this system by the natural environment. Although most economists have recognized that the environment is a resource not accounted for in dominant economic practice, fewer have recognized that our narrative conceptions of the environment depend just as completely on an exploitation of the real environment. We borrow from the real environment, so to speak, when we build an image of the environment that allows to ignore fundamental responsibility for environmental protection. That is, our narrative environment, our narrative environmental paradigm, must now essentially be understood also as a story that does not quite work.

Can there be hope for realistic social action for environmental progress through the mass media? This is a complex question. In our view, however, media institutions tend to stack the deck against positive social change. Yet, social change does occur, and does so despite the media. Where does such social change come from if it is not motivated by media attention to issues?

The answer is actually rather simple. Environmentalism is a spontaneously generated social movement and derives its energy from sources having little to do with mass media or other institutions that uphold the DSP. Here, we speak not of the "public" environmentalism but of the private encounter we all eventually face with the ultimate reality. Each of us eventually comes to see something of the shallowness associated with the postmodern media culture and imagines that a narrative with a more faithful connection to an authentic reality must exist. The NEP is not this narrative, however, because what we all seek in the end has little to do with a social paradigm. Indeed, our nature-narrative struggle eventually comes to rest on our determined need to search for something that is extra-social, something out of the human sphere, so to speak. Even the characteristically effective messages of the mass media cannot remove this human need. That is, all of us, while cngagcd in thc human processes of social existence, struggle to experience the nonhuman as one ground or foundation for human existence. No social forces need to motivate this tendency, which in itself is "natural." Thus, we think a meaningful agenda for socioenvironmental action comes not from the overthrow or replacement of old social paradigms but from a realization of this connection we all seek. To understand that human characterization of the environment is not the final answer on environmental issues is perhaps the most important decision we can make. Advocacy of an NEP does not solve the problem; it postpones it to a different level.

Here, we return to Evernden (1992) who argued that our social and narrative activities tend to rob nature of one of its most important qualities: that of being "other."

> Our children learn from "educational" television that nature is machinery, and the boundary between flesh and electronics is hopelessly blurred. The "otherness" that is required in development will now be of our own making, and therefore not genuinely other at all. (p. 116)

The end of nature? Probably not, but if Evernden, McKibben, and others are correct, we have reached a very important watershed point in our experience with nature. Evernden continued:

In the face of any phenomenon, we have a choice between
explaining or accepting it. If the former, then we have not seen
it, for it becomes just "one of" something else, nothing but
another instance of the same old thing. (p. 117)

Thus, it begins to look as if environmental problems take on
a religious cast, which is certainly the direction authors such as
McKibben (1994) would take us.

Can media effectively portray environment as "other"? This
seems to us unlikely. Although suggesting an agenda for social
action is difficult given the dimensions of the problem, we think
that those committed to environmental protection and action
should begin to consider media roles in the environmental problem
more explicitly, rather than accidentally. Social movements have
tended to assume that media coverage of their activities is essential
for real social action in today's environment. But that may not be
entirely true. If those committed to social action on environmental
issues want to make progress toward a truer and more realistic
environmental narrative, they may well wish to consider fundamentally disconnecting themselves from mainstream media institutions. Although that will make communication more difficult in the
short term, it could facilitate longer term change for sustainability.

REFERENCES

Ader, C. (1993). *A longitudinal study of agenda setting for the issue of environmental pollution.* Kansas City, MO: Association for Education in Journalism.

Ader, C. (1995). A longitudinal study of agenda setting for the issue of environmental pollution. *Journalism and Mass Communication Quarterly, 72*(2), 300-311.

Allen, C., & Weber, J. (1983). How presidential media use affects individuals' beliefs about conservation. *Journalism Quarterly, 60,* 98-104.

Althoff, P., Greig, W., & Stuckey, F. (1973). Environmental pollution control attitudes of media managers in Kansas. *Journalism Quarterly, 50,* 666-672.

Atwater, T., Salwen, M., & Anderson, R. (1985). Media agenda setting with environmental issues. *Journalism Quarterly, 62*(2), 393-397.

Bachmair, B. (1991). From the motor-car to television: Cultural-historical arguments on the meaning of mobility for communication. *Media, Culture, and Society, 13,* 521-533.

Backes, D. (1995). The biosocial perspective and environmental communication research. *Journal of Communication, 45*(3), 147-163.

Bailey, G. (1970). The public, the media, and the knowledge gap. In A. Schoenfeld (Ed.), *Interpreting environmental issues* (pp. 237-242). Madison, WI: Dembar.

Banerjee, S., Gulas, C., & Iyer, E. (1995). Shades of green: A multidimensional analysis of environmental advertising. *Journal of Advertising, 24*(2), 21-31.

Barnouw, E. (1970). *A history of broadcasting in the United States* (Vol. 3). New York: Oxford.

Barthes, R. (1957). *Mythologies*. New York: Hill & Wang.

Barton, R. (1988). TV news and the language of acid rain in Canadian-American relations. *Political Communication and Persuasion, 5*(1), 49-65.

Bell, A. (1994). Media (mis)communication on the science of climate change. *Public Understanding of Science, 3*, 259-275.

Berger, P., & Luckmann, T. (1966). *The social construction of reality*. New York: Anchor.

Berry, T. (1988). *The dream of the Earth*. San Francisco: Sierra Club Books.

Bormann, E. (1982). A fantasy theme analysis of the television coverage of the hostage release and Reagan inaugural. *Quarterly Journal of Speech, 68*, 133-145.

Bormann, E. (1985). Symbolic convergence theory: A communication formulation. *Journal of Communication, 35*(4), 128-138.

Bowman, J., & Fuchs, T. (1981). Environmental coverage in the mass media: A longitudinal study. *International Journal of Environmental Studies, 18*, 11-22.

Bowman, J., & Hanaford, K. (1977). Mass media and the environment since Earth Day. *Journalism Quarterly, 54*, 160-165.

Brightman, R. (1987). Conservation and resource depletion: The case of the boreal forest Algonquins. In B. McCay & J. Acheson (Eds.), *The question of the commons: The culture and ecology of communal resources* (pp. 121-141). Tucson: University of Arizona Press.

Brother, C., Fortner, R., & Mayer, V. (1991). The impact of television news on public environmental knowledge. *Journal of Environmental Education, 22*(4), 22-29.

Bryant, J., & Zillmann, D. (Eds.). (1994). *Media effects: Advances in theory and research*. Hillsdale, NJ: Erlbaum.

Burgess, J. (1989). The production and consumption of environmental meanings in the mass media: A research agenda for the 1990s. *Transactions of the Institute of British Geography, 15*, 139-161.

Burgess, J., & Harrison, C. (1993). The circulation of claims in the cultural politics of environmental change. In A. Hansen (Ed.), *The mass media and environmental issues* (pp. 198-221). Leicester, UK: Leicester University Press.

Burgess, J., Harrison, C., & Maiteny, P. (1991). Contested meanings: The consumption of news about nature conservation. *Media, Culture, and Society, 13,* 499-519.

Burke, K. (1945). *A grammar of motives.* New York: Prentice-Hall.

Cottle, S. (1993). Mediating the environment: Modalities of TV news. In A. Hansen (Ed.), *The mass media and environmental issues* (pp. 107-133). Leicester, UK: University of Leicester Press.

Cracknell, J. (1993). Issue arenas, pressure groups, and agendas. In A. Hansen (Ed.), *The mass media and environmental issues.* Leicester, UK: University of Leicester Press.

Dark, A., & MacArthur, L. (1996). *Native Americans and the environment.* New Haven, CT: http://www.indians.org/library/biblio.html

DeHaven-Smith, L. (1988). Environmental belief systems. *Environment and Behavior, 20*(2), 176-199.

DeHaven-Smith, L. (1991). *Environmental concern in Florida and the nation.* Gainesville: University of Florida Press.

Downing, J. (1988). The alternative public realm: The organization of the 1980s anti-nuclear press in West Germany and Britain. *Media, Culture, and Society, 10,* 163-181.

Downs, A. (1972). Up and down with ecology—The "issue attention cycle," *The Public Interest, 28,* 38-50.

Dunlap, R. (1992). Trends in public opinion toward environmental issues: 1965-1990. In R. E. Dunlap & A. Mertig (Eds.), *American environmentalism: The US environmental movement, 1970-1990.* Philadelphia: Taylor & Francis.

Dunlap, R. (1995). Public opinion and environmental policy. In J. P. Lester (Ed.), *Environmental politics and policy: Theories and evidence* (pp. 63-114). Durham, NC: Duke University Press.

Dunlap, R., & Mertig, A. (1992). *American environmentalism: The US environmental movement, 1970-1990.* Philadelphia: Taylor & Francis.

Dunlap, R., & Scarce, R. (1991). The polls—poll trends: Environmental problems and protection. *Public Opinion Quarterly, 55*(4), 651-672.

Dunlap, R., & Van Liere, K. (1984). Commitment to the dominant social paradigm and concern for environmental equality. *Social Science Quarterly, 65,* 1013-1028.

Dunwoody, S., & Griffin, R. (1993). Journalistic strategies for reporting long-term environmental issues: A case study of three Superfund sites. In A. Hansen (Ed.), *The mass media and environmental issues.* Leicester, UK: University of Leicester Press.

Easterbrook, G. (1995). *A moment on the earth.* New York: Viking.

Einsiedel, E., & Coughlan, E. (1993). The Canadian press and the environment: Reconstructing a social reality. In A. Hansen (Ed.), *The mass media and environmental issues* (pp. 134-149). Leicester, UK: University of Leicester Press.

Eisler, R. (1987). *The chalice and the blade.* San Francisco: HarperCollins.

Erfle, S., McMillan, H., & Grofman, B. (1989). Testing the regulatory threat hypothesis: Media coverage of the energy crisis and petroleum pricing in the late 1970s. *American Politics Quarterly, 17*(2), 132-152.

Evernden, N. (1992). *The social creation of nature.* Baltimore, MD: Johns Hopkins University Press.

Fanfare fades but awareness, actions, increase. (1994, April 21). *Boston Globe*, p. 1.

Fink, E. (1990). Biodegradable diapers are not enough in days like these: A critique of commodity environmentalism. *EcoSocialist Review, 4*(2).

Fisher, W. (1984). Narration as a human communication paradigm: The case of public moral argument. *Communication Monographs, 51.*

Fisher, W. (1985). The narrative paradigm: In the beginning. *Journal of Communication, 3,* 74-89.

Fisher, W. (1987). *Human communication as narration: Toward a philosophy of reason, value, and action.* Columbia: University of South Carolina Press.

Fisher, W. (1988). The narrative paradigm and the interpretation of historical texts. *Argumentation and Advocacy, 25,* 49-53.

Fortner, R., & Lyon, A. (1985). Effects of a Cousteau special on viewer knowledge and attitude. *Journal of Environmental Education, 16*(3), 16-24.

Fortner, R., & Wiggington, M. (1989). Natural history programming on television: A comparison of markets. *Journal of Environmental Education, 21*(1), 15-18.

Fox, S. (1985). *The American conservation movement.* Madison: University of Wisconsin Press.

Friedman, S., Gorney, C., & Egolf, B. (1987). Reporting on radiation: A content analysis of Chernobyl coverage. *Journal of Communication, 37*(3), 58-69.

Funkhouser, G.R. (1973). Trends in media coverage of the issues of the 1960s. *Journalism Quarterly, 50,* 533-538.

Gale, R. (1987). Calculating risk: Radiation and Chernobyl. *Journal of Communication, 37*(3), 68-79.

Gerbner, G., & Gross, L. (1976). Living with television: The violence profile. *Journal of Communication, 26*(2), 173-199.

Gerbner, G., Gross, L., Morgan, M., & Signorielli, N. (1981). Scientists on the TV screen. *Culture and Society, 42*, 51-54.

Gerbner, G., Gross, L., Morgan, M., & Signorielli, N. (1982). Charting the mainstream. *Journal of Communication, 32*(2), 100-127.

Gerbner, G., Gross, L., Morgan, M., & Signorielli, N. (1994). Growing up with television: The cultivation perspective. In J. Bryant & D. Zillmann (Eds.), *Media effects: Advances in theory and research* (pp. 17-41). Hillsdale, NJ: Erlbaum.

Gerbner, G., Gross, L., Signorielli, N., & Morgan, M. (1980). Aging with television: Images on television drama and conceptions of social reality. *Journal of Communication, 30*(1), 37-47.

Gillroy, J., & Shapiro, R. (1986). The polls: Environmental protection. *Public Opinion Quarterly, 50*, 270-279.

Gitlin, T. (1982). Media sociology: The dominant paradigm. *Mass communication review yearbook* (pp. 50-73). Beverly Hills, CA: Sage.

Gorney, C. (1992). Numbers versus pictures: Did network television sensationalize Chernobyl coverage? *Journalism Quarterly, 69*(2), 455-465.

Gray, D. (1985). *Ecological beliefs and behaviors: Assessment and change.* Westport, CT: Greenwood.

Greenberg, M., Sachsman, D., Sandman, P., & Salamone, K. (1989). Risk, drama, and geography in coverage of environmental risk by network TV. *Journalism Quarterly, 66*(2), 267-276.

Griffin, R. (1989). Communication and the adoption of energy conservation measures by the elderly. *Journal of Environmental Education, 67*(3), 19-28.

Griffin, R. (1990). Energy in the eighties: Education, communication, and the knowledge gap. *Journalism Quarterly, 67*(3), 554-566.

Gronbeck, B. (1983). Narrative, enactment, and television programming. *Southern Speech Communication Journal, 48*, 229-242.

Gross, L. (1984). The cultivation of intolerance: TV, blacks, and gays. In G. Melischek, K. Rosengren, & J. Stappers (Eds.), *Cultural indicators: An international symposium* (pp. 345-363). Vienna: Verlag der Osterreichischen Akademie der Wissenschaften.

Hall, S., Cruchter, C., Jefferson, T., Clarke, J., & Roberts, B. (1978). *Policing the crisis.* London: Macmillan.

Hansen, A. (1991). The media and the social construction of the environment. *Media, Culture, and Society, 13*, 443-458.

Hansen, A. (1993a). Greenpeace and press coverage of environmental issues. In A. Hansen (Ed.), *The mass media and environ-*

mental issues (pp. 150-178). Leicester, UK: University of Leicester Press.

Hansen, A. (1993b). *The mass media and environmental issues.* Leicester, UK: University of Leicester Press.

Hepburn, M., & Hepburn, L. (1985). Case study of the acid rain film controversy: Political propaganda or environmental education. *Journal of Environmental Education, 16*(4), 1-6.

Hilgartner, S., & Bosk, C. (1988). The rise and fall of social problems: A public arenas model. *American Journal of Sociology, 94*(1), 53-78.

Hilts, P. (1988, December 8). Some greenhouse effects: Pestilence, super-storms? *Washington Post,* p. A4.

Howenstine, E. (1987). Environmental reporting: Shift from 1970 to 1982. *Journalism Quarterly, 64,* 842-846.

Jacobs, R. (1996). Producing the news, producing the crisis: Narrativity, television, and news work. *Media, Culture, and Society, 18,* 373-397.

Kempton, W. (1991, June). Lay perspectives on global climate change. *Global Environmental Change,* pp. 183-208.

Kempton, W., Boster, J., & Hartley, J. (1995). *Environmental values in American culture.* Cambridge, MA: MIT Press.

Krimsky, S., & Plough, A. (1988). *Environmental hazards: Communicating risk as a social process.* Dover, MA: Auburn House.

Kuhn, T. (1962). *The structure of scientific revolutions.* Chicago: University of Chicago Press.

LaMay, C., & Dennis, E. (1991). *Media and the environment.* Washington, DC: Island Press.

Larson, M., Zimmerman, D., & Scherer, C. (1982). Communication behavior by environmental activist compared to non-active persons. *Journal of Environmental Education, 14*(1), 11-20.

Lasch, C. (1975). *Haven in a heartless world.* New York: Basic Books.

Lazarsfeld, P., & Merton, R. (1971). Mass communication, popular taste, and organized social action. In W. Schramm & D. Roberts (Eds.), *Processes and effects of mass communication* (pp. 554-578). Urbana: University of Illinois Press.

Lewis, M. (1992). *Green delusions.* Durham, NC: Duke University Press.

Lippmann, W. (1922). *Public opinion.* New Brunswick, NJ: Transaction.

Lomatuway'ma, M., Lomatuway'ma, L., & Namingha, S. (1993). *Hopi ruin legends.* Lincoln: University of Nebraska Press.

Lovelock, J. (1995). *Gaia: A new look at life on Earth.* Oxford: Oxford University Press.

Lowe, P., & Morrison, D. (1984). Bad news or good news: Environmental politics and the mass media. *Sociological Review, 32*(1), 75-90.

Lull, J. (1986). Ideology, television, and interpersonal communication. In G. Gumpert & R. Cathcart (Eds.), *Inter/media: Interpersonal communication in a media world* (pp. 597-610). New York: Oxford University Press.

Mander, J. (1991). *In the absence of the sacred: The failure of technology and the survival of the Indian nations.* San Francisco: Sierra Club Books.

Mazur, A., & Lee, J. (1993). Sounding the global alarm: Environmental issues in the US national news. *Social Studies of Science, 23,* 681-720.

McComas, K. (1994). *NAPAP's blind spot.* Unpublished master's thesis, Boston University, Boston.

McKibben, B. (1989). *The end of nature.* New York: Random House.

McKibben, B. (1992). *The age of missing information.* New York: Random House.

McKibben, B. (1994). *The comforting whirlwind: God, Job, and the scale of creation.* Grand Rapids, MI: Eerdmans.

McLeod, J., Glynn, C., & Griffin, R. (1987). Communication and energy conservation. *Journal of Environmental Education, 18*(3), 29-37.

McLuhan, M. (1964). *Understanding media.* New York: Anchor Books.

Meadows, D. (1991). Changing the world through the information-sphere. In C. LaMay & E. Dennis (Eds.), *Media and the environment* (pp. 67-79). Washington, DC: Island Press.

Meyrowitz, J. (1985). *No sense of place: The impact of electronic media on social behavior.* New York: Oxford University Press.

Mikami, S., Takeshita, T., Nakada, M., & Kawabata, M. (1995). The media coverage and public awareness of environmental issues in Japan. *Gazette, 54,* 209-226.

Moore, D. (1995). Public sense of urgency about environmental issues wanes. *The Gallup Poll Monthly, 3,* 17-20.

Morgan, M. (1982). Television and adolescents' sex role stereotypes: A longitudinal study. *Journal of Personality and Social Psychology, 43*(5), 947-955.

Morgan, M. (1987). Television, sex role attitudes, and behavior. *Journal of Early Adolescence, 7*(3), 269-282.

Morgan, M. (1990). International cultivation analysis. In N. Signorielli & M. Morgan (Eds.), *Cultivation analysis.* Newbury Park, CA: Sage.

Morgan, M., Alexander, A., Shanahan, J., & Harris, C. (1990). Adolescents, VCRs, and the family environment. *Communication Research, 17*(1), 83-106.

Morgan, M., & Gross, L. (1980). Television viewing and reading. Does more equal better? *Journal of Communication, 30*(1), 159-165.

Morgan, M., & Shanahan, J. (1991a). Do VCRs change the TV picture. *American Behavioral Scientist, 35*(2), 122-135.

Morgan, M., & Shanahan, J. (1991b). Television and the cultivation of political attitudes in Argentina. *Journal of Communication, 41*(1), 88-103.

Morgan, M., & Shanahan, J. (1992). Comparative cultivation analysis. In F. Korzenny & S. Ting-Toomey (Eds.), *Mass media effects across cultures* (pp. 173-197). Newbury Park, CA: Sage.

Morgan, M., & Shanahan, J. (1996). Two decades of cultivation research: An appraisal of meta-analysis. *Communication Yearbook, 20*, 1-45.

Morgan, M., Shanahan, J. & Harris, C. (1990). VCRS and the effects of television: New diversity or more of the same. In J. Dobrow (Ed.), *Social and cultural aspects of VCR use*. Hillsdale, NJ: Erlbaum.

Morgan, R. (1992). The Earth had its day last week. *Adweek Eastern Edition, 33*, 52.

Nash, R. (1982). *Wilderness and the American mind*. New Haven: Yale University Press.

National Opinion Research Center (1994). *General Social Surveys, 1972-1994: Cumulative codebook*. Storrs, CT: Roper Center.

Nimmo, D., & Combs, J. (1982, Winter). Fantasies and melodramas in television network news: The case of Three Mile Island. *The Western Journal of Speech Communication, 46*, 45-55.

Norusis, M. (1993). *SPSS professional statistics*. Chicago: SPSS.

Novic, K., & Sandman, P. (1974). How use of mass media affects views of solutions to environmental problems. *Journalism Quarterly, 51*, 448-452.

Oelschlager, M. (1991). *The idea of wilderness: From prehistory to the age of ecology*. New Haven, CT: Yale University Press.

Ostman, R., & Parker, J. (1986/1987). A public's environmental information sources and evaluations of mass media. *Journal of Environmental Education, 18*(2), 9-17.

Ostman, R., & Parker, J. (1987). Impact of age, education, newspapers, and television on environmental knowledge, concerns, and behaviors. *Journal of Environmental Education, 19*(1), 3-9.

Patterson, P., & Wilkins, L. (1990). Risky business: Covering slow-onset hazards as rapidly developing news. *Political Communication and Persuasion, 7*, 11-23.

Pearce, W. (n.d.). *Forms of communication*. Unpublished document.

Pearce, W. (1989). *Communication and the human condition*. Carbondale: Southern Illinois University Press.

Pirages, D., & Ehrlich, P. (1974). *Ark II: Social response to environmental imperatives*. San Francisco: Freeman.

Planet of the year. (1989, January 2). *Time* [Special issue], *133*(1).

Ploman, E. (1980). Information as symbolic environment. *Intermedia, 81*(3), 21-22.

Potter, W.J. (1994). Cultivation theory and research: A methodological critique. *Journalism Monographs*, 1-35.

Price, J. (1995). Looking for nature at the mall: A field guide to the Nature Company. In W. Cronon (Ed.), *Uncommon ground: Toward reinventing nature*. New York: Norton.

Protess, D., & McCombs, M. (Eds.). (1991). *Agenda setting: Readings on media, public opinion, and policymaking*. Hillsdale, NJ: Erlbaum.

Rice, R., & Atkin, C. (1994). Principles of successful communication campaigns. In J. Bryant & D. Zillmann (Eds.), *Media effects: Advances in theory and research* (pp. 365-387). Hillsdale, NJ: Erlbaum.

Rifkin, J. (1988, July 31). The greenhouse doomsday scenario. *Washington Post*, p. C3.

Rodman, J. (1983). Ecological sensibility. In D. Scherer & T. Attig (Eds.), *Ethics and the environment* (pp. 88-92). Englewood Cliffs, NJ: Prentice-Hall.

Rogers, E., & Dearing, J. (1988). Agenda-setting research: Where has it been, where is it going? *Communication yearbook* (Vol.11, pp. 555-594). Beverly Hills, CA: Sage.

Ross, S. (1991). Proud to be speciesist. *New Statesman and Society, 4*(148), 21-22.

Rothschild, N. (1987). Cohesion and control: Relationships with parents as mediators of television. *Journal of Early Adolescence, 7*, 299-314.

Salamone, K., Greenberg, M., Sandman, P., & Sachsman, D. B. (1990). A question of quality: How journalists and news sources evaluate coverage of environmental risk. *Journal of Communication, 40*(4), 117-130.

Sandman, P., Weinstein, N., & Klotz, M. (1987). Public response to the risk from geological radiation. *Journal of Communication, 37*(3), 93-108.

Scammon, D., & Mayer, R. (1995). Agency review of environmental marketing claims: Case-by-case decomposition of the issues. *Journal of Advertising, 24*(2), 33-43.

Scheaffer, R., Mendenhall, W., & Ott, L. (1990). *Elementary survey sampling*. Boston: PWS-Kent.

Schoenfeld, A. (1979). The press and NEPA: The case of the missing agenda. *Journalism Quarterly, 56*, 577-585.

Shabecoff, P. (1983, October 21). Haste of global warming trend opposed. *The New York Times*, p. 1.

Shabecoff, P. (1986, June 11). Swifter warming of globe foreseen. *The New York Times*, p. 17.

Shabecoff, P. (1988a, March 29). Temperature for world rises sharply in the 1980s. *The New York Times*, p. 1.

Shabecoff, P. (1988b, June 26). Calculating the consequences of a warmer planet Earth: A worst-case forecast. *The New York Times*, p. 1.

Shanahan, J. (1992, March). *Green but unseen: Marginalizing the environment on television*. Paper presented at the Mainstream(s) and Margins meeting, Amherst, MA.

Shanahan, J. (1993). Television and the cultivation of environmental concern. In A. Hansen (Ed.), *The mass media and environmental issues* (pp. 181-197). Leicester, UK: University of Leicester Press.

Shanahan, J. (1996). Green but unseen: Marginalizing the environment on television. In M. Morgan & S. Leggett (Eds.), *Margin(s) and mainstreams: Cultural politics in the 90s* (pp. 176-193). Westport, CT: Greenwood.

Shanahan, J., & McComas, K. (1997). Television's portrayal of the environment: 1991-1995. *Journalism and Mass Communication Quarterly, 74*(1), 147-159.

Shanahan, J., Morgan, M. & Stenbjerre, M. (1997). Green or brown? Television's cultivation of environmental concern. *Journal of Broadcasting and Electronic Media, 41*, 250-268.

Shrum, L., McCarty, J., & Lowrey, T. (1995). Buyer characteristics of the green consumer and their implications for advertising strategy. *Journal of Advertising, 24*(2), 71-82.

Signorielli, N., & Morgan, M. (1990). *Cultivation analysis*. Newbury Park, CA: Sage.

Simon, J. (Ed.). (1995). *The state of humanity*. Cambridge, MA: Blackwell.

Singer, E. (1990). A question of accuracy: How journalists and scientists report research on hazards. *Journal of Communication, 40*(4), 102-117.

Singer, E., & Endreny, P. (1987). Reporting hazards: Their benefits and costs. *Journal of Communication, 37*(3), 10-26.

Singer, S. (1992). In J. Lehr (Ed.), *Rational readings on environmental concerns* (pp. 393-403). New York: Van Nostrand Reinhold.

Singletary, M. (1994). *Mass communication research: Contemporary methods and applications*. White Plains, NY: Longman.

Stevens, W. (1993, September 14). Scientists confront renewed backlash on global warming. *The New York Times*, p. 1.

Suhonen, P. (1993). Environmental issues, the Finnish major press, and public opinion. *Gazette, 51,* 91-112.

Sullivan, D. (1985). Comprehensiveness of press coverage of a food radiation proposal. *Journalism Quarterly, 62*(4), 832-837.

Thomashow, M. (1995). *Ecological identity: Becoming a reflective environmentalist.* Cambridge, MA: MIT Press.

Trafzer, C. (1993). Grandmother, Grandfather, and the first history of the Americas. In A. Krupat (Ed.), *New voices in Native American literary criticism.* Washington, DC: Smithsonian Press.

Trumbo, C. (1994, April). *Inter-media agenda-setting and the issue of global warming: A time series analysis.* Paper presented at the AEJMC conference on media and the environment, Reno, NV.

Trumbo, C. (1996). Constructing climate change: Aims and frames in US news coverage of an environmental issue. *Public Understanding of Science, 5,* 269-283.

Ungar, S. (1992). The rise and relative decline of global warming as a social problem. *The Sociological Quarterly, 33*(4), 483-501.

VanDeVeer, D., & Pierce, C. (Eds.). (1986). *People, places, and plastic trees.* Belmont, CA: Wadsworth.

Waters, F. (1963). *Book of the Hopi.* New York: Penguin.

Weigel, R., & Weigel, J. (1978). Environmental concern: The development of a measure. *Environment and Behavior, 10,* 3-15.

White, L., Jr. (1967, March 10). The historical roots of our ecological crisis. *Science,* pp. 1203-1207.

Wiebe, G. (1973). Mass media and Man's relationship to his environment. *Journalism Quarterly, 50,* 426-432.

Wilkins, L. (1990). Taking the future seriously. *Journal of Mass Media Ethics, 5*(2), 88-101.

Wilkins, L. (1993). Between facts and values: Print media coverage of the greenhouse effect, 1987-1990. *Public Understanding of Science, 2,* 71-84.

Wilkins, L., & Patterson, P. (1991). *Risky business: Communicating issues of science, risk, and public policy.* Westport, CT: Greenwood Press.

Winett, R. A., Leckliter, I. N., Chin, D. E., & Stahl, B. (1984). Reducing energy consumption: The long-term effects of a single TV program. *Journal of Communication, 34,* 37-51.

AUTHOR INDEX

SUBJECT INDEX